Where the Swallowtail Kite Soars

Photo: *Courtesy of Bud Adams, The Adams Ranch, Ft. Pierce, Florida*

GLADES COUNTY, FLORIDA
WHERE THE SWALLOWTAIL KITE SOARS

Where the Swallowtail Kite Soars

❖

The Legacies of Glades County, Florida
and
The Vanishing Wilderness

Nancy Dale

iUniverse, Inc.
New York Lincoln Shanghai

Where the Swallowtail Kite Soars
The Legacies of Glades County, Florida and The Vanishing Wilderness

iUniverse, Inc.

For information address:
iUniverse, Inc.
2021 Pine Lake Road, Suite 100
Lincoln, NE 68512
www.iuniverse.com

Edited by Annalane Harris
Cover design by Nancy Dale
Author contact: www.nancydalephd.com
Cover photograph: Bud Adams, The Adams Ranch, Fort Pierce, Florida

ISBN: 0-595-32557-2 (pbk)
ISBN: 0-595-66641-8 (cloth)

Printed in the United States of America

Contents

PREFACE

Florida ranch history and the people who made it, is captured by Nancy Dale. In today's world, the value of a ranch is much more than pounds of beef. Its value is a home to families, a place for wildlife, an employment opportunity, a healthy watershed, a tax base for schools, and a link to our history.

New pioneers are still riding horses and grazing cattle, but today they are using computers, cell phones, and DNA tests to produce cattle that are adapted to the area, and produce the high quality beef our market demands.

Bud Adams
The Adams Ranch Ft. Pierce, Florida
2004

With appreciation

To Gregory Lasanta, my son, who has always encouraged me to follow my dreams.

To Annalane Harris, my sister/editor and nephew Scott who have always supported my intangible endeavors.

To Pattie Parker, Miami Jackson High School Swingette, who has held the light and laughter for more than 50 years.

To John "Who Watches the Grass Grow" who inspired me to pursue this epic journey.

ACKNOWLEDGEMENTS

In traveling through the many lives and stories in writing this book, the experience goes beyond the text and research.

To those along the way who offered time, encouragement, wisdom and foresight in moving this project to completion, I am deeply grateful.

Special thanks to: Bud Adams for his magnificent photos of nesting Swallowtail Kites; Samantha Davis (Ft. Pierce Utilities Authority) for her originality in web page construction; Don Landin (Ft. Pierce Utilities Authority); Matthew Lachance (MJ Computerware), whose technical expertise deciphered this conglomeration of materials, and took it from the computer to the printed page; John and Kim Farrabee who drew "the outsider" into their circle; Minnie Mae (who said it was O.K. to ride across the Everglades prairie with a cowboy); Patty Register (Gatorama); Debra Miller and Katrina Elsken of the Glades County Democrat. A special thanks to Mamie and Leroy Boyce (Leroy deceased) who were always there for me in Palmdale, keeping alive my little "silver bullet" refuge for all these years.

During the last hot days of summer, a special note of appreciation to those who conceived the Big O bike path and the preservation of one of Florida's ancient swamps at Highland Hammocks State Park where I spent many contemplative bike rides writing this book in my head. To the nice people at Brewski's, a cool, dark roadside grill in Okeechobee where I enjoyed a good home cooked meal, beverage, serenity and anonymity. To those who silently wondered what I was writing, this is it.

To the many Palmdale locals whose path I crossed over the years at the little red shoebox Oasis in the prairie, the General Store, the campground, the pond, Volpe's, the cookouts at the community center or Ray Hendry's blue grass festivals, thanks for the memories.

This book is for you.

To the Reader....

Exploration into the unknown inspires the human spirit and heightens curiosity. It is an adventure for those who dare to search for the secrets of life burrowed within life itself. It is a never ending discovery and challenge wedging the imagination between time and space, to pluck the small wisdom we might therein discern with our limited understanding of who we are and where we are going.

This small missile is a reflection of Glades County pioneers at the turn of the century; it is only a small fraction of the lives that sowed the seeds of today. This saga of historical events occurred over 100 years and serve as a barometer for the next stage; the subject of another book and a history, sadly, that will never turn back the pages to the "good old days" of Glades County.

The new Glades County pioneers hold the key to the future, however it may be written.

Nancy Dale

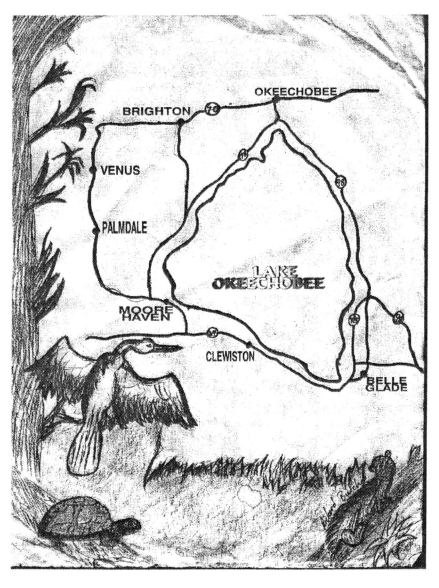

Map of Lake Okeechobee
Artwork by Richard Butcher, student, St. Lucie West Centennial High School

INTRODUCTION

Twenty to ten thousand years ago when the last Ice Age began to retreat, straggly haired hunters wearing the skins of their trophies crossed over Berengia, the icy land bridge from Siberia, tracking giant mastodons to the bottom of the Earth into the peninsula of Florida. When the Paleo-Indians of the late Pleistocene Epoch migrated to Glades County, it was barren and dry unlike the lush cabbage palm prairies and cypress swamps that exist today. But, all that remains of the ancient ones' struggle to survive the unpredictable, unforgiving natural forces of the Everglades are fossilized bones, giant animal skulls impaled with spears, and mound villages scattered across Glades County.

Since those ancient times, many explorers have made their way to Glades County and survived. Some pioneers paddled their way down Fisheating Creek in hand-carved canoes, rode atop hand-sewn leather saddles, traveled the rails of the Hinky Dinky or drove shiny black Tin Lizzies on muck-rutted trails, each bringing with them their satchel of dreams.

In the 1900's, Otto Fog laid out his plan to create a "Garden of Eden" in Palmdale. At the center of the town was the picturesque Palmdale Hotel with verandas sporting tall silk hats atop groomed, dapper tourists on the arm of ladies clad in egret feathered bonnets, satin dresses gracing wide-open porches reaching over tannic cypress swamps. What remains of those dreams and the majestic hotel are a few wooden pine frames wrought together by hardened sap and rock, unmarked, unknown.

New people will continue to make their way to Glades County and discover this last pristine wilderness nestled on the soft green shoulder of Lake Okeechobee. But, with Florida's exploding population, and an increased demand for land and water, is it possible to preserve the vanishing wilderness and keep the land alive?

Those pioneers who survived the hurricanes, droughts, black clouds of mosquitoes, cottonmouth moccasins, rattlesnakes, alligators and the swamp, learned to live in harmony with the land that gave them life. There is no other place on Earth like the pristine wilderness of Glades County. The whispering fans of tall cabbage palms, ancient cypress trees grabbing the ceiling of the Earth, and Fisheating Creek meandering through the heartland, become "one" with those who linger here as long as time allows.

This book is an endeavor over several years, to research and record the legacies of Glades County pioneers so that their way of life, their dreams, hopes, struggles, laughter and hard earned lessons will not be forgotten. Although these pages may yellow and ink fade, the pioneer spirit recorded here will forever live in those inspired by their lives, who dare to pin their hope upon a star and follow their own dreams into the wilderness.

The beauty that magnetized the early settlers to endure the elements of time and Nature still prevails in Glades County. The castanets of crickets and chirping frogs can still be heard along Fisheating Creek, once in a while a shy Florida Panther can be spotted fleeting through thick palmetto patches, and overhead the Swallowtail Kite still soars.

"Blue Sky"—Swallowtail Kites on Nest

Photo: *Courtesy of Bud Adams, The Adams Ranch, Ft. Pierce, Florida*

1

FLORIDA'S PRIMORDIAL HISTORY: PALEO-INDIANS HUNT ANCIENT MASTODONS IN GLADES COUNTY

Some 65 million years ago before the Earth froze, reptilian domination came to a close, ushering in the Cenozoic Epoch, or "Age of Recent Life."

Maybe it was an anomaly scientists speculate dates back to the Cenozoic Era some 23 million years ago, when every 100,000 years an eccentricity of the Earth's orbit alters its trajectory from circular to elliptical around the sun, brushing the planet closer to the blazing solar fire. Whatever spun the planet into the sun's hot flashes thousands of years ago, the Earth reacted with dramatic climatic changes. Searing equatorial heat swept over the northern half of the planet, splitting the Earth's crust, sucking up water from every pore and baking the planet in relentless soaring temperatures. Then, as if to protect itself from dying, the skin of the Earth shivered in chilblains triggering transient glaciation, drawing a massive blanket of crystalline ice over its blistering surface, shrouding North America in a frozen shield. The massive ice bore trenches into the Earth, carved out the Great Lakes with mile deep glaciers, horded fresh water and lowered sea levels as virgin landmasses, buried millions of years in the ocean's depths, slowly began to rise.

Throughout the Pleistocene Epoch of "The Great Ice Age," 1.8 million years ago, ice impeded southward sweeping cold air over the continent for the next million years. At the southern most tip of North America, hardly noticed in its geological time, a tiny thumb in the sea composed of millions of marine coquina shells and limestone powdered with sugar sand was dredged up from its oceanic tomb to dry out in the first light of the blazing sun. The mostly dry terra firma of the little peninsula was defined with shapely indentations of inland and upland coasts. Hendry County, west of the second largest body of fresh water in North America, Lake Okeechobee sunk into the center of the state, flaunted shimmering white beaches stretching 50 miles into the shallow tropical sea of the Gulf of Mexico drenching the southern half of the peninsula.

At the curve of its northern spine, the peninsula and its chiseled coastal terraces slopping into the ocean, remained sturdily anchored to North America despite a rocking sea of fluctuating shorelines rising and sinking over eons of geological time.

THE GREAT ICE AGE RETREATS

The turbulent Earth changes continued another half million years. Then, eleven thousand years ago, glaciers north of the Great Lakes began a very fast meltdown. Warming temperatures sheered off massive ice sheets, deluging rivers and steams with fresh water, chiseling canyons and valleys rushing towards the open sea. Sea levels rose 100 feet, inundating coastlines, taking back low lying land into the watery grave from wince it came. The phosphorous rich waters that flowed over Central Florida left behind sediment that solidified into phosphate nodules holding onto the remains of marine life layered with a Bone Valley of pre-historic animals and phosphorus rich deposits beneath Bartow, Florida, northwest of Glades County.

THE MELTDOWN

The glacial water gushed southward filling Florida's thirsting underground aquifers, sinking into porous limestone, enriching the crusty terrain with soil. The soil multiplied in nutrient rich deposits, giving life to a mosaic of low-lying xeric vegetation, punctuated with a primordial forest over the exposed continental shelf. "The Ice Age" over North America continued to expand and retreat throughout the late Pleistocene Era of the Paleo-Indian Period (3 million-10, 000 years ago).

Meanwhile, in the frozen Arctic, a 100-mile wide land corridor emerged linking the two massive continents. It was over this jagged, natural bridge scientists named "Berengia" that the first people, following an intrinsic human instinct to discover "what was over there," crossed from the great Siberian tundra into the future of North America.

TRACKING THE GIANT MASTODON TO FLORIDA

Over twelve thousand years and many generations, the Paleo-Indians hunted and foraged their way into the Southwest and Florida.

Adapting to drier climatic conditions, the Paleo-Indians competed for survival alongside the lumbering vegetarian mastodon, giant sloths, bison, and herds of saber tooth tigers, siphoning scarce freshwater from limestone wells, devouring a portion of life offered up from the land.

Central Florida's vast low-lying plains, rivers and gentle sloping coasts offered ideal grazing territory for small and large vegetarians and a vast hunting ground for the Indians. The long, gigantic frame of the wooly mastodon towered more than 30 feet over the frail humans but the Indians were not intimidated; they hunted the beast almost to extinction. The fiercest meat-eating predator who proved to be the most successful hunter in the territory was the two-legged Paleo-Indian possessing human intelligence and a lancelet missile.

THE HUMAN PREDATORS

The ingenuity of the new people was their key to survival. They studied the competition and invented technology to compensate for their diminutive size and frailness against the giants, carving piercing needle nosed weapons out of stones quarried from riverbeds. They shaped the stones into razor sharp missiles secured at the tip of spears. During the perpetual hunt for food, warmth and shelter, the natives stalked along meandering rivers where giant beasts sunk their heavy bodies into cool Artisan springs, vulnerable and unsuspecting of the clever, quick hunters. With the stealth of brave warriors, the Indians sprang upon their prey, impaling it in their most tender part as the beast struggled to free its burdened body from the suctioning river muck.

Roaming across the Florida heartland was the thirty-six toothed armadillo with hundreds of razor sharp scoots armored on its leathered back; the 500 pound, eight foot beaver with upper incisors that were more than ten inches in length. There were herds of camels, thick wooly bison, gentler deer and tapirs (a semi-aquatic animal with a long, flexible nose like an elephant's trunk that hunted among the mega fauna), all living beneath a canopy of more than 267 species of birds, whose fragile remains are difficult to classify today. The giant creatures possessed the grassy plains and crusted coastal terrain of Central Florida, ruling the peninsula for the next 12,000 years.

As the giant creatures died off during the interglacial period of the late Pleistocene Epoch, the Caloosahatchee Formation in Central Florida became a major depository of fossilized life. Submerged in sandy tombs of limestone outcrops in sinkholes and river runoffs were solidified bones of lost species and discarded remains strewn over the Paleo-Indian hunting grounds baring evidence of butchering and human activity. Like a witches' brew of parts and layers of time, giant mastodon tusks were unearthed north of Glades County at Wakulla Springs. West of the county at Little Salt Spring (Sarasota County), a 13 thousand-year-old giant tortoise was found still impaled with an ancient wooden spear. Unearthed in Glades County was a fossilized whale skull the size of a compact automobile, along with assorted shark teeth, vertebrate and a camel leg bone all heaved together and deposited some 1.7 to 2 million years ago, long before the arrival of the first humans in Florida.

By the late Pleistocene (8,000 B.C), the last of the giant mammals that co-existed with Paleo-Indians in Glades County finally became extinct, wiped out by catastrophic climatic change and the finely honed hunting skills of the humans.

Primordial cypress forest

As global warming continued, Florida was covered with dark green forests swallowing up low-lying scrub grasslands where huge herds of animals foraged and hunted. In Glades County, Fisheating Creek curved through large exotic ferns, lush pine and oak forests providing secretive hiding places along the water's edge for the smaller mammals and reptiles that replaced the former giants. Glades County's rich "black gold" soil and plentiful water was ready for the human "agronomists."

2

THE INDIAN MOUND VILLAGES IN GLADES COUNTY

THE REMAINS OF THE "SOCIOTECHNOLOGISTS" OF THE ARCHAIC PERIOD (8,000 B.C. TO 750 B.C.) ORTONA AND LAKEPORT (FT. CENTER)

Living in a Florida twice the size it is today, the Paleo-Indian hunters survived 3,000 years adapting and subsisting in an emerging wetland camping along fresh water rivers in over a hundred sites. Over the last eight to six thousand years, the aboriginal Indians settled down in more permanent encampments and learned how to farm. It was in the Calhoosahatchee River Basin of the Big Cypress Swamp that the nomadic hunters became agriculturalists.

The upper Caloosahatchee River Valley rises gently to the north and south with western boundaries of the watershed sloping downward across the low-lying Silver Bluff terrace of Central Florida to the coast. Five million years ago, the Caloosahatchee watershed was part of the shallow tropical Gulf of Mexico that flooded the lower peninsula.

The physiology of the Caloosahatchee River Valley is influenced by a subtropical climate pattern, sharply delineating wet and dry seasons in the southern watershed, fluctuating more climatically to the north. The interaction between climate and physiology with a self-regulating seasonal pattern responding to cycles of flood or drought was ideal for early agriculturalists to grow basic crops.

The wet season allowed excess water from streams to soak into the soil and replenish aquifers beneath the watershed. During the dry season, surface water levels receded and stored water flowed through rivers and surrounding wetlands.

The watershed created a livelihood for the first human settlers with a plentiful and varied diet.

The early Indians are described by some archeologists as "sociotechnologists," the first people in Glades County to design villages around agricultural development. They created mound villages with processes for draining ditches and ponds in order to plant crops, utilizing natural resources to sustain their existence. The ancient mound villages are scattered across Glades County, but two of the major developments have been studied and one preserved.

3,000 YEARS AGO: ORTONA—THE LONGEST CANALS IN NORTH AMERICA

Today, traveling north on U.S. Highway 27 to Moore Haven, at the tip of Lake Okeechobee and turning onto State Road 78 west, the sign leads to the entrance of the Ortona Mounds Historic Site. Some 3,000 years ago, the Indians who settled on one of the highest ridges in Glades County, later named Ortona (after 20th Century founder's Italian birth place) are believed to have brought with them agricultural adaptations from South America. It is speculated that the Ortona settlers may have been related to the early Calusa (Calos) Indians or "Fierce People" whose vast warrior empire ruled the southern coastal areas of southwest Florida's Ten Thousand Islands. (It was the Calusas' that attacked Ponce de Leon when he landed in their northern territory, wounded him and forced his return to Cuba where he died).

The Adizoo or Ortona Indians left evidence of their cultural heritage as mound builders, agriculturalists, traders, craftsmen and river navigators. The Adizoo, or "people," molded fine earth ware from the sand, creating colorful and intricate designs reflecting their artistic nature. The people lived a life of fishing and hunting, mainly eating a diet of turtle and deer, cultivating gourd and cucurbits (similar to a pumpkin) in their agrarian gardens. Palmetto berries and wild plants were plentiful on the island of pine, scrub oak and swamp (before it was drained in the 20th Century). The mounds, scattered over five square miles on the north side of the Caloosahatchee River, are one of the largest preserved sites in Florida. There is no explicit evidence to determine why the Indians built mounds except to protect their houses from the rising water table that gradually flooded the flat prairie.

The Ortona site reveals evidence of a complex society of ancient Indians. They cultivated maize (corn) and stored it seasonally to equalize their food supply. Pollen analysis indicates that they may also have cultivated squash and beans. They devised a technique to alter the Savannah topography carving circle ditches to drain fields for planting and utilized the ditch spoils as a possible source of fertilizing mulch. By acquiring tools and adaptive skills, they were able to shape their lives around the natural resources of the Caloosahatchee River Valley in order to survive.

The Adizoo also developed a waterway trade route at Ortona using the then network at Charlotte Harbor for passage up the Caloosahatchee through some of the longest canals in North America. They meandered in their wooden canoes through wet prairies and over waterfalls linked to larger channels. One of these series of canals connected Pine Island to the Caloosahatchee River and Cape Coral through Lake Okeechobee, thus making these people the first humans to create a river route to the Lake. Today, many of these ancient Everglades river trails through which the Adizoo and Calusa poled their hand-carved canoes are "dead rivers." The ancient waterways have either been drained or dried up.

When the Adizoo vanished from Ortona, they left behind great pieces of earthen art partially hidden in thick palmettos, vulnerable for thousands of years to looters, pothunters, construction of the nearby Ortona cemetery roadbeds and sand mining business that plundered much of these Adizoo treasures in the 1930–50's. What remains at Ortona is a huge temple mound surrounded by a protective boardwalk constructed by the Glades County Historical Society to preserve the site.

Although the early Indian mound builders have vanished, Florida's agricultural industry springs from the same rich basin of "black gold" soil that sustained the ancient agronomists.

How long the "blue gold" water and land will remain pristine for future "socio-technologists" is an unknown history in Florida's future.

LAKE PORT: THE OLD WORLD MOUND BUILDERS OF THE BELLE GLADE CULTURE—FT. CENTER (CA. 750 B.C. to A.D. 1500)

By 1000 B.C., another aboriginal population settled at what is called "Ft. Center" on Fisheating Creek at Lakeport (a small community skirting U.S. Highway

78 on the west side of Lake Okeechobee). The vast Savanna around Lake Okeechobee, called Lake Mayaimi, was part of the developing Belle Glade Culture.

The Belle Glade Indian settlers declined the nomadic lifestyle to become agriculturalists. They surveyed the land, its resources, its hydrology, physiology and created manmade systems to survive. The Belle Glade people were mound builders. They dug ditches and created complex geometric shapes for their villages, growing small amounts of maize that is believed (as well as the Adizoo at Ortona), to have been brought with them from South America.

The Belle Glade Indian mounds on Fisheating Creek were stumbled upon by "dredge men" plundering archeological finds around Ft. Center. The "dredge men" were construction workers hired to dredge the land of water for the growth of the citrus and cattle industry. (Ft. Center was a Union fortification founded during the 1800 Seminole Indian Wars as a base of operation to remove the native Indians from Florida).

In 1962, Lykes Brothers, Inc. (a multi-national citrus/cattle business in Glades County) that owns the land where the mounds are situated was having difficulty keeping trespassers and treasure hunters from the remote site. Lykes Brothers budgeted money for an archeological investigation of the Ft. Center Mounds by Dr. William H. Sears. Florida Atlantic University, professor emeritus of anthropology who recorded his findings in *Fort Center, an Archeological Site in the Lake Okeechobee Basin.*

LIVING IN A MOUND VILLAGE

Ft. Center Indian Mounds were occupied for over 2,000 years. The site is divided into two areas, four phases of ceremonial and habitational occupation. The mounds were built in groups and some arranged in geometric patterns. In the early settlement, the mound-pond complex was ceremonial with mounds used as burial sites and mounds called "kitchen middens," composed of shells and animal bones, broken pottery and tools. The mounds built up as high as 30 feet over generations of occupation.

Dr. Sears' research reveals between Burial Mound B and Midden A there was a 40-foot deep pond. It is speculated that the pond furnished sand to build the mounds and was used as a garbage disposal. On the top of layers of debris, bones of about 100 individuals were deposited along with animal skulls, deer and carved items.

The pit pond had apparently been used also as a "charnel house" or house of the dead, evidenced by bones bundled with arrows, spears, and carved objects placed on a platform above the water. When the platforms collapsed, everything sank to the bottom of the pond. The pond was re-filled again and again over time. When each new generation reclaimed the mounds, the remains of its former human habitants were retained at the bottom of the pit.

Pits and trenches of various sizes were placed in low mounds in several parts of the complex possibly dug for drainage. Ditch basins were excavated below the hardpan to allow water to drain, drying the surrounding area. Earthwork finds indicate that the villagers organized the planting of food crops in linear and circular fields to allow for more convenient harvesting.

There is a term used by archaeologists as a "Sun Circle." The "Sun Circle" is constructed with a circular canal three or four feet deep with rising banks about the same height. The canals are fifty feet across the top with a diameter running a quarter of a mile. Inside the "Sun Circle" is a circular elevation of six small mounds spaced equally apart. The base of the mounds is encircled by a wide, deep trench with four to five foot high embankments and the midden or kitchen area lying beyond the wall. The Fort Center circle was rebuilt at least two times, the second rebuilding increasing its area from 300 to about 1200 feet.

Dr. Sears and his team classified and preserved artifacts including gracefully carved ceramic wooden birds on a platform structure suggesting that the birds were a totem or religious symbol. One hundred or more fragments of mostly pine wooden figures were found at the site.

The Belle Glade people made tools from flint as well as from stone, shell, and shark's teeth. The shark's teeth were used to hone delicate fine detail on ornaments for headdresses, belts and ear lobes. Fossils from the early Pleistocene Period were also unearthed at Ft. Center believed to have been washed up on the higher ground and used by the Belle Glade culture a million years later.

The Belle Glade Indians were craftsmen. They hammered thin, heavy slabs of silver combined with copper to create artistic designs and to form ornamental shark's teeth. Some of the metal specimens unearthed were from Spanish origin, suggesting that Spanish captives may have been used to melt and cast the silver objects.

Archeologists believe that Ft. Center Mounds in its later rebuilding phase is part of the sixteenth- and seventeenth-century Calusa Empire, noting changes in ceramics and ornaments uncovered at the site.

Within 200 hundred years of the Spanish invasion of Florida in the 1500's, the great Calusa Empire became extinct. (In 2004, researchers discovered the first birth records of Calusa Indians in Cuba that may substantiate that the tribe was not completely wiped out. Anthropologist John Worth said several Calusa Indians that lived in southwest Florida from 100 A.D. to the early 1700's, escaped to Cuba after the Spanish invasion. Records trace one surviving infant from the tribe.) The Ft. Center site of the Belle Glade people was abandoned by A.D. 500 due to increasingly wet conditions.

A TOMBSTONE OF ROAD BEDS AND PALMETTOS FOR THE DEAD

The unmemorialized, unmarked remains of the Ft. Center Indian Mounds—Lakeport

The Belle Glade Indian mounds off Banana Grove Road on State Road 78 is now part of the State of Florida's Wildlife Management Area and remains an unmarked rise across from the site where old Fort Center used to stand. The area, covered with palmettos and oaks, can only be spotted with the trained eye of Fish and Wildlife Biologist Grant Steelman. Knowledge of the mounds and their existence on the elevated plateau can only be discovered in the pages of books or at the Florida Museum of Natural History in Gainesville. There is no monument to distinguish the mounds or its cultural existence, yet adjoining the site, under the Management District's permissible recreational usage area, the wake and roar of airboats part the saw grass at the oxbow of Fisheating Creek.

PRESERVATION OF MOUND VILLAGES IN FLORIDA

Just as the plundering of the Belle Glade/Ft. Center mounds, other archaeological remains of past cultures continue to be destroyed by looters, or uninformed agricultural and commercial developers in other areas of Florida. Beginning in the late nineteenth century, commercial mining destroyed many of the large pre-Columbian shell heaps—archaeological sites—found around Tampa Bay and the central portion of the St. Johns River drainage. The shells dug from sites were used to pave the roads in many Florida towns.

In South Florida, other treasures, such as those on Biscayne Bay in Miami, fell in the twentieth century to the construction of hotels, homes, and businesses. Mounds were bulldozed for fill dirt and backhoes dug peat from ponds in which people buried their dead thousands of years ago. As elsewhere in the United States, there is little protection for the past in contrast to many other countries where the past is considered part of a national heritage that belongs to all and must be carefully managed for future generations.

However, on the east coast of Florida, a large Indian mound unearthed at the old site of Florida Institute of Technology in Martin County will be preserved as a cultural monument. The Southeast Florida Archeological Society plans to convert a building in Riverside Park to an archeological center of statewide significance. The park is the home to a 4,000 year-old Indian mound as well as a network of other archeological sites. Investigations indicate that the artifacts may predate the construction of the Egyptian pyramids and the site may have served as the center for an immense Pre-Columbian chiefdom. The Indian Riverside Park Advisory Board, the Martin County Board of Commissioners, the Martin County Parks and Recreation Dept, the Historical Society of Martin County and the Indian Riverside Alliance support the project. The site will also establish out-door excavation teaching units to instruct Martin County school children and the public. The plans also call for a center with books, materials and other inter-active programs. "To Walk through Time," exhibit will take visitors on a Plexi-glas trail of an Indian mound to give visitors insights into the earliest cultures in North America. The park will be developed in stages; a pavilion is set for con-struction as the first phase of an eco-tourism attraction to create an Indian artifact museum around the mound site.

Perhaps the Ft. Center Site, which is presently unmarked and basically unknown, can one day be a trademark for ecotourism and the cultural preservation industry evolving in Glades County. In 1999, the Economic Development Council in Glades County was working on the final stages with Gulf Coast University to develop a Strategic Management Plan incorporating the development of clean industry with eco- and cultural heritage tourism to maintain the wilderness areas and expand a sustainable economy in Glades County.

Before the Ft. Center mounds could be preserved in the 1960's, Dr. Sears believes that much of the original structure was already comprised. The mounds, believed to have spanned over 200 feet in diameter with 20-foot high walls were scrounged out and flattened by looters.

500 YEARS AGO: THE BEGINNING OF CULTURAL EXTINCTION

The complex societies of the Calusa, Ocale, Apalachee are a few of the Florida Indians who carved a lifestyle from the Everglades swamp, co-existing with a menagerie of reptiles and wild panthers, enriching their lives off the plethora of replenishable natural resources. With the shorelines moving in during the later Archaic (ancient period 9,000 BP to Pre-Ceramic period 6500–2000 BC), the sea became a primary food source for early Indians. They began to adapt their toolmaking to fishing, using a flint like stone called chert to make a variety of small tools. In Lee County, 80 miles to the west of Glades County, the early peo-ple left behind fishhooks, harpoon points and dugout canoes.

As European exploration began to conquer the oceans, the New World exploita-tion began the final phase of the downfall of the indigenous people. The Spanish and French sought to colonize the State with Ponce de Leon establishing the first non-native permanent settlement in North America at St. Augustine on September 8, 1565, some 50 years after his arrival in Florida.

When Ponce de Leon arrived, there were approximately 350,000 Indians of the Calusa, Ocale, and Apalachee tribes inhabiting the peninsula that encountered Spaniards up until the sixteenth century. However, the early native agronomists and traders, blighted with the onslaught of foreign cultures, stopped their mound building and adapted to the introduction of new products. As European explorers established trade with villagers and built Missions, they also brought with them smallpox, measles and mumps that spread rampantly throughout the villages taking their toll on the Indians who had no resistance to the foreign strains of disease. Within 250 years of the Europeans arrival, Florida Indians were becoming extinct.

As further European colonization continued to bring settlers to North America, Indian tribal land to the north in Alabama and Georgia was threatened to be absorbed by the new world explorers. The birth of the Seminole Tribe in Florida and Glades County was the outcome of early Indians being forced to leave their native lands or fight to the death. In an attempt to remain free, various Indian tribes began to migrate southward uniting with other tribes in the Everglades to live off the land and preserve their cultural heritage. The birth of the Seminole Nation, rich in pride and reserve, reflects the sorrows, courage and tears woven into the history of a people who settled in Glades County.

3

A TRAIL OF COURAGE AND TEARS: THE SEMINOLE TRIBE IN GLADES COUNTY

◆

BRIGHTON

In the late 1700s, the history of Florida's Seminole Indian Tribe is traced to the end of the American Revolution in a "Trail of Courage and Tears." The initial confrontations between the U.S. government and Native Indians began when Indians inhabited vast open land in Alabama, Georgia and Northern Florida. As European colonists continued to arrive up and down the Atlantic Coast, the native Indian land was targeted for settlement. The United States attempted to purchase the land from the Euchee, Yamasee, Timugua, Tequesta, Balachi, Coca and other tribes living in these areas but many refused to sell.

Historically, it was the Maskoki tribe in Alabama who were the first to challenge the onslaught of "foreigners" attempting to push the Natives off the land and other Indian tribes that supported "white" settlers (Creek War of 1813–14). General Andrew Jackson forced a treaty on the Creeks and took 2 million acres of land away from the Natives after illegally entering Spanish Florida and massacring Indian inhabitants. This was the First Indian War in Florida between 1814–18. When the Maskoki people were dispossessed of their land, they began the long and arduous migration southward, packing up children and their lean possessions to join forces with a mixture of other Indians the Europeans called "Seminoles" hiding deep in the Florida swamps.

In Florida, three Seminole Wars occurred between unsettled treaties, described by Seminole historians as not protecting the rights of the Native people. By 1820, before Florida became a U.S. Territory, there were at least 5,000 Seminoles, Creeks and Maskoki people living on the peninsula. In Maskoki, the core language, "isti siminoli" means "free people," or as Stanlo Johns, Cattle Manager of the Brighton Seminole Reservation translates, as "wild people." English speakers garbled the Hitachi dialect with Maskoki and called all Indians "Seminoles" not acknowledging the distinction of original tribal heritage.

The Second Seminole War (1835–42) was costly. It was also said to be the first "guerilla" style warfare fought by U.S. troops prior to the Viet Nam conflict. Colonel William S. Harney (namesake of Harney's pond on Hwy 78 who was the first person to use a six-shooter in Florida) claims that he learned his "open field," hit-and-run fighting tactics from the fierce Seminole Indians. One soldier wrote home after a grueling encounter with Indians in the Everglades: "If the Devil owned both hell and Florida, he would rent out Florida and live in Hell."

In 1841, President John Tyler ordered the end of military actions against the Seminoles, $20 million later with a death toll of 1, 500 American soldiers and 3,000 Natives removed to the West. After an unsteady truce, the third and last confrontation between Seminoles and U.S. soldiers was in 1856 when a team of Army surveyors where sent to the Everglades to capture a powerful Seminole called Abiaka.

Abiaka was one of three legendary Seminole leaders, Osceola (William Powell), Billy Bowlegs, and medicine man Abiaka (Sam Jones). Abiaka's role was to create "medicine," or stir warriors into a frenzy as the Seminole historians describe it. He directed several battles, including the 1837 ambush known as the Battle of Okeechobee. Abiaka would not surrender or compromise with the U.S. government, resisting the removal of Indians from inhabited lands. His last camp was in the Big Cypress Swamp where he remained, surrounded by troops, until he starved to death. Upon the hallowed ground of the Big Cypress, Abiaka's legend still brims with spiritual powers today.

Another famous Seminole, Osceola, masterminded successful battles against U.S. generals, murdered a United State's Indian Agent, and punished those who associated with the "white man." Osceola represents the legendary Seminole image of resistance, never signing a peace treaty with the United States. Osceola was captured and died in a Charleston, South Carolina prison in 1838.

The Third Seminole War was led by an honored figure in Glades County, Seminole Billy Bowlegs. The three-year battle against the government ended with a withdrawal of troops but no treaty or victory. War torn, fatigued but not defeated, the remaining Seminoles withdrew deeper into the Everglades to live off of the natural resources in no-man's land, a place where soldiers dared not to trek.

State Road 78 Monument to Billie Bowlegs

As the 20th Century approached and Florida was once again flooded with new settlers from all over the world, the tourist industry began to spread its roots. According to historians, many Seminoles were living in poverty, hiding out in remote Everglades camps and still living off the land. They chose a way of life that intentionally had little contact with the outside world except for hunting, trapping, fishing and trading at frontier outposts to earn income.

In the 1920's, Florida's "boom days" brought land developers by rail and "Tin Lizzies" into Glades County (then part of DeSoto County). The majestic Palmdale Hotel arose from the swamp, as well as the Chicago Land Company's Citrus Center Hotel (off of Highway 78) further south, to host potential buyers seeking a wilderness adventure. Many Seminoles began to work in "the wage economy" at the hotels and in the growing agricultural industry. The birth of the tourist industry also provided a stage for a unique survival skill of the Seminole. Alligator wrestling. The Seminole women also entered the market economy, selling their intricately designed jackets and jewelry at nearby stores and county fairs.

THE RESERVATIONS

In 1934, Congress passed the Indian Reorganization Act, recognizing the right of American Indians to conduct elections and govern their own political affairs by constitution and by-laws. By 1938, the Federal Government set aside 80,000 acres of land for Seminole reservations at Big Cypress, Hollywood and Brighton offering Native Indians an agricultural based economy. Holding firm to an independent spirit, few Seminoles moved onto the reservation.

At the end of World War II, the government attempted to reduce federal costs by targeting the Bureau of Indian Affairs (BIA) and federal services to some Native American tribes. The termination of federal aid to the Florida Seminoles was announced in 1953. Cut off from federal assistance, the Seminoles had to either return to the old ways of living off the land, or learning a new way to maintain their independence in a market economy. On August 21, 1957, the Seminoles voted to establish an administrative entity called the Seminole Tribe of Florida; however, not all Seminoles voted to participate in the newly formed organization.

The tribe, whose heritage was living off the land, hunting and fishing now was expected to enter the free enterprise system with little training in administrative and management skills. However, this did not deter the Seminole leaders from their effort to establish a self-sustaining economy. With staunch self-determination Seminole leaders began to educate themselves in business creating the roots of the Tribe's own educational system.

On August 21, 1957, the Seminoles on the Hollywood, Big Cypress and Brighton Reservations led the adoption of a Charter and Constitution by democratic vote. Representing Brighton Reservation was Billy Osceola and Toby Johns; Big Cypress, Josie Billie and Jimmie Cypress. The group traveled to Washington to assist in the formation of the new Seminole Tribe of Florida. The Seminole Tribal Council replaced the traditional Council of Elders and the corporate charter of the Seminole Tribe of Florida, Inc. was approved.

Today, the Council administers the Tribal gaming enterprises, citrus groves, the Billie Swamp Safari and the Ah-Tah-Thi-Ki Museum. Many of the non-reservation Miccosukee tribe, residing alongside Tamiami Trail west of Miami, still live in thatched palm huts constructed by their ancestors during the Indian Wars as easily assembled and dismantled sleeping platforms for warriors to escape an ambush by U.S. soldiers deep into the night.

At the Brighton Reservation, Stanlo Johns says the people still live close to Nature. Matter of fact, Tribal members express the belief that if the land dies, so will the Tribe. One of the enterprises besides the Brighton Casino operated at Brighton is their cattle industry. Johns says 42 families own the cattle herd with approximately 5,000 head of mother cows. However, in order to sustain itself, the reservation must have enough grass, water, fertilizer and feed to support their cattle and citrus economy. This is a predominate concern of Stanlo Johns at the Brighton operation as well as other agribusinesses around Lake Okeechobee with the encroachment of land development from all points north, south, east and west also requiring land and water.

Stanlo Johns, Cattle Manager Brighton Seminole Reservation

"BRING YOUR OWN WATER, GAS AND RESOURCES IF YOU COME TO FLORIDA"

Johns says that two big arteries from Lake Okeechobee pass through the reservation at Harney Pond and Indian Prairie. As a party to the Seminole Land Claims Settlement Act of 1987, the Tribe transferred the land and water rights to the State as part of the historic Big Cypress State reservation to be managed by the Water Management District for Everglades restoration. The action expanded State holdings in the environmentally sensitive water conservation Area 3A as part of the Everglades Protection Area. The tribe is also part of the Everglades Restoration Initiative, a multi-year project initiated in 1999 that impacts the quality and quantify of water flowing off the Big Cypress Reservation into the Everglades.

Stanlo Johns says that the Water Management District (under the West Palm Beach jurisdiction) "doesn't want to pump out but so much water from Lake Okeechobee." He says there is "a conflict between sports fishermen who want the lake to be lower where grass breeds brim and bass. The Seminoles created a water compact signed in the 70's by local users that was designed to monitor water usage and water quality." He says, "The major polluters and negative impact on users of Lake Okeechobee is not the agribusiness but the urban users as far away as Ft. Lauderdale and their increased demand for water." Johns suggests, "The solution to keeping the Lake alive is to have people migrating into South Florida be prepared to bring in their own water, gas and other resources that the land cannot presently sustain."

In the Tribe's development, the Seminoles have historically been charged with finding their own sustainable industries in order to survive. They used their ingenuity and deep understanding of the natural environment to carve a living from the land. There is a deeply rooted connection to the present that is ironically a reminder of the past: Early Native Indians were rousted from their inhabited lands when federal mandates determined the fate of the Indians. The government forced restrictions on the Indians that dispossessed them of their land and the ability to provide for their economic self-reliance.

At the turn of the Century, the Bureau of Indian Affairs started shipping cattle to the Indians; they built an industry. Johns says the Seminole initiative continues to pursue a new business venture in Glades County: aquaculture. In 1988, the Seminoles started catfish farming, but were unable to supply the demand over the

12-year period of the business. Johns says that "there are not enough Native people to run all of the enterprises, and often, some of the young Indians seem to lack the initiative to support a market economy." Johns observes "the 35 years he has lived at the reservation that the Native culture is slipping away. It takes two parents to keep a family economically alive in a fast world. It is difficult to transfer one hundred years of myths and stories to the youth, and revive the old ways when an adopted cultural work ethic of a market based economy requires 8 to 12 hours on a job disconnected from the Land." Johns believes the Seminoles "are losing their heritage and their language. A lot of the young people do not speak the native tongue. Even those special people, who are eligible to train for the rigorous life of a 'Medicine Man,' have diminished in number. In order to be eligible for a Medicine Man, one must be 'great,' and live up to very rigid standards, requiring a solitary life."

Stanlo Jones does not forget the lessons of the old Medicine Men that speak to morals and ethics through animal stories. Johns remembers one enigmatic tale that asks: "Why are there no lions in the country? The rabbit had something to do with it; the lion eats the rabbit in a heartbeat."

Stanlo Johns grew up in an isolated area called Blue Field near Ft. Pierce on the east coast of Florida, speaking only Miccosuki the first ten years of his life. As his family migrated around Florida following work, he became a calf roper and bareback rider. Stanlo Johns is a Veteran, as are many other Seminoles, born on the Fourth of July, 1935.

THE BRIGHTON SEMINOLES: CLANS, MEDICINE MEN AND THE FUTURE

There are few other more pageantry historical legends then that of Florida's Seminole Indians. One might not think of a trail of courage and tears as "pageantry," but the splendid traditions, cultural heritage and magnificent stories of courage and bravery that the Seminoles have kept alive and died for represent an indomitable spirit of a People not forgotten.

The clan system is tied closely to the traditional dances. The clan system has been recorded since the beginning of time and controls the dances. The dancers keep the Spirit of the clan. The dances are a reminder of the Tribe's closeness to nature, the Land that Stanlo Johns "feels is being lost by expanding economic cultural values."

Each Seminole is born into the clan of the mother. There are eight clans: Panther, Bear, Deer, Wind, Bigtown, Bird, Snake and Otter. You are not allowed to marry within the clan. When the last female dies, the clan is said to be extinct. The Panther clan is the largest of the Seminole Tribe of Florida. During the Green Corn Dance that symbolizes a purification and manhood ceremony, clans play an important role. Men and women separate into different "camps" according to their clans. The Medicine Man leads the males in a stomp dance, while the women shuffle with them.

The quiet reserve of the Seminoles is not as demonstrative in their ceremonial rights as other native tribes. The expression of gratitude to the Creator, and resolving internal disputes are more private and exclusive to traditional tribal practices. The details of the medicine culture are also not discussed outside of the Tribe.

The Seminoles entered Florida's thriving tourism market featuring the male's prowess at alligator wrestling and the sale of beautifully crafted patchwork garments designed by the women. Even though many of the native people were influenced by European dress in the early 1700's, the Seminoles still express their heritage through the hand sewing of traditional costumes. The beautiful feminine flowing skirts worn by the women with strings of glass beads are a traditional garment. It is said that a Seminole baby gets its first strand of beads at birth and every year thereafter. Then at mid-life, until the end, a strand of beads is removed until the last given to the woman at birth is removed at death.

The males typically wear a turban made from plaid with a full cut shirt adorned with colorful ruffles and symbols. The symbols relate to the land and are painstakingly stitched together. Some of the symbols represent rain, fire, the broken arrow, bird, four directions of medicine colors, the crawfish, tree, diamondback rattlesnake and bones. Take note, the next time you wear one of the colorful Seminole jackets.

The Brighton Seminole Tribe is a unique part of Glade's County history. The contribution of their rich heritage is one to be appreciated. Their courage and fortitude to hold onto their culture is admirable in a rapidly changing world where old values appear to be less important than fast cars, money and creature comforts. Although the Brighton tribe has become more involved in the market economy, they strive to maintain a respect for the old ways. Some people still live in the traditional palm thatched dwelling or "chickee" and wear traditional garments just as did their ancestors two centuries ago.

PRESERVING A CULTURAL HERITAGE IN A TECHNOLOGICAL AGE

The Brighton Tribe entered the market economy in order to become self-sufficient developing, the citrus enterprise, tourism, gambling, rodeos, arts and crafts, aquaculture (turtles) and the Brighton Seminole Campground. The Brighton Citrus Grove, established in 1984 began with 40 acres of land intended to only serve the community. In 1999, the grove has expanded into a variety of citrus types cultivated on 150 acres and is profitable. They plan to add an additional 85 acres of land that increases the size of the grove to over 235 acres with plans for future expansion. The BIA has also offered a grant for technical assistance to determine the possible leasing of other citrus groves if soil conditions are desirable.

As the Seminole historians express, the Tribe's strongest desire is to maintain economic independence and uphold their proud reserve, resilience and self-reliance ever present in their stature and manner. Even though Stanlo Johns says we are just like "any other people," he carries a heritage on his sleeve, depicted in the patchwork symbols of his vest, in the quiet reserved strength that underscores his words as he speaks about the Tribe. The Seminoles are not just like any other people; their heritage is special in the price, they too, have paid for freedom. The Seminole culture has survived despite the battle scars and persecution. They are a proud and sensitive people. They did not give into weakness or betrayal. They persevered into the 21st Century and gained their independence.

The Seminoles stand as a reminder to others who have endured difficult hardships that the resiliency of the human spirit does not die. Through adaptation, bravery, and courage, one can overcome the ever-present negative forces in society; even transform the negative into a positive reality with relentless Will.

Modernization, technology and the inanimate "things" of the world will always be a temptation for the youth to turn their backs on their ancestors, but in the end, everyone looses. The sense of being a "non-person" is an easy "persona" to adapt and may be rewarded with material gain. However, the question that arises in studying the staunch and courageous history of the Seminole Tribe is what internal forces in man's Nature spurs him to resist accepting and adopting the vast emptiness of prefabricated values around every corner in today's society?

Perhaps society's transformation from a violent form of communication to an "idealistic" view of a positive future outlook comes down to the core of each individual. Perhaps the opportunity for transforming society is dependent upon each person's examination of their own individual "courage" in the everyday world, to strive to live values that nourish the human spirit with a sense of appreciation for the beauty in life that may sometimes become blurred and taken for granted.

Living in an increasingly complex world challenges the strongest to remain true to one's self, age-old values of respect for the Earth and each individual. Human beings may be facing a different challenge in order for humanity to survive, the challenge to confront the issues of society in a different way than violence and negativity. The Warrior Spirit in each person may be characterized in a new way, as summarized in an old Indian saying: "There is nothing so strong as gentleness, nothing so gentle as real strength."

The wilderness surrounding Lake Okeechobee and in Glades County is rich in natural wonder. All one really has to do is look up at the stars at night to understand the vast amazing universe in which the life of the planet lives. Hopefully, space science will not dazzle and blind the human eye with man made objects that obscure Man's wonderment of the natural world. Technology and modernization is a wonderful "thing," but they are just that. Sitting down with a Seminole Indian, such as Stanlo Johns, having a conversation, watching gut-wrenching cowboys battle bucking bulls, or looking up through a coal black sky at the scattering of stars blanketing the Universe, puts one back in touch with a different essence of life that is not forgotten. This Spirit of real life reminds one of the magical essence within each person that has transformed the world since time immemorial. Lest we forget!

4

1900's
THE GRADUAL
EXTINCTION OF THE
FLORIDA COW HUNTER

✦

CITRUS CENTER

1948—L to R: Woodrow and Billy Peeples, Joe Hogan, Sr., Bo Pearce, Joe
Peeples and Jimmy Hargrove
Citrus Center

LEGENDARY COW HUNTER—DONALD PEEPLES

The Peeples' clan is part of Florida's cow hunter folklore. Donald and Dorothy Peeples live in a modest ranch house that lies amidst miles of Everglades prairie. However, now instead of the rough, tough scrub cattle believed to be brought in by early Spanish explorers that were the first cattle herd of Joe Peeples, Sr., (Donald's dad) the land is spotted with Brahmans, Angus, Herefords and Charlois as far as the eye can see.

The history of the Peeples family in America stretches back to the 1600's when David "Peebles" arrived from Scotland. Peebles had to escape England during the English Scottish Wars or else be beheaded by Lord Cromwell for opposing English rule in Scotland. Eventually, some of the Peebles, who later spelled their name "Peeples," settled in Virginia, the Carolinas and Georgia. Their background varied from doctors, to farmers to attorneys and cattlemen. In 1869, William Hosea Peeples migrated to Ft. Mead, Bowling Green and Wauchula, Florida after serving in the Confederate Army.

In the early 20's, Joe Henry Peeples, Sr. moved from Arcadia to Crewsville, Venus and Palmdale to Citrus Center to raise "scrub cattle." The scrub cattle were the only cows that survived through adaptation to droughts, freezes, starvation, and floods typical in the early days of then despot land before the draining of the Caloosahatchee that squeezed some of the water out of the saturated soil.

Joe Peeples, Senior, Donald's father, was a man who learned early how to best utilize the natural resources in the inhospitable Everglades environment. The Peeples' were one of the early pioneering cattle families around Lake Okeechobee along with Bud Adams, Buck King (his daughter Zoe King married Tom Lykes and eventually sold his cattle business to Lykes), the Lykes Brothers, the Carltons', the Summerlins', and Whiddens'.

In 1928, Joe Peeples, Sr. was elected to the County Commission and served almost continuously until his death in 1943. According to old issues of the Glades Democrat, Peeples was 21 when he became Tax Collector for DeSoto County, served on the Glades County Commission, and was later elected to the State Legislature. Some of the causes he supported include: the opposition to netting prohibitions in the early fishing industry; local control of drainage districts versus the State; he worked to prohibit the construction of future levies on Lake Okeechobee with flood control taxes; he worked to gain the Governor's veto to cancel Glades County's hurricane relief debt that would have had to be paid by the Glades taxpayers already struggling to survive from the onslaught of droughts, floods, during the Depression. Joe Peeples, Sr. also lobbied against confining livestock and any efforts to build fences. After Joe Peeples, Sr. died, his son Joe Peeples, Jr. who was already in the cattle business at age 13 continued in his father's footsteps supporting similar legislation. He served as a Glades County Commissioner for many years until his retirement.

Joe Hogan, Sr. and Joe Peeples

Joe Peeples, Sr. raised W. H. (Billy) Peeples, Dorothy, Joe, Woodrow and Donald around Citrus Center. W. H. Peeples was born in Citrus Center when it was just a crook in the road. The family worked together raising the small herd of scrub cattle for market where they were sold around eight years old, not a "spring chicken" for today's cattle market, then driven by cow hunters across the state to Punta Rassa near Ft. Myers where that were sold to Cuba. These were the days when there were no fence laws and huge migratory cattle drives gave impetus to the developing cattle business on unimpeded "cracker" trails across Central Florida. However, in 1930, the rangeland was fenced in an effort to eradicate the rapidly spreading fever tick even though in 1917, voluntary "dipping" had begun at Boars Hammock and Citrus Center in an attempt to rid the cattle of the pest. Matter of fact, it was much later in 1948 during dipping time, that a perky young lady, Dorothy caught the eye of Donald Peeples during a trip to visit her aunt

Annie Padget. Dorothy, who lived in Illahaw, Florida, helped Donald dip cattle in the arsenic tick formula during her stay at Citrus Center. After a week she returned home but the "love bug" had bitten! Four months later Dorothy returned to Citrus Center and married Donald. On January 26, 2000, the couple celebrated 51 years of marriage.

As time passed, Donald Peeples says the scrub cattle mostly disappeared or were mixed with Brahmans, except for a few known herds called "cracker cows" inheriting the last of the gene pool. The horses that worked the scrub cattle also became known as "cracker horses," due to their shorter legs and hardy breeding. Always accompanying the cow hunter was his trusty "cur dog" that learned to snap at the cattles' noses to get them moving. The cur dog, according to Donald Peeples, is a cross between a bulldog and a red bone hound.

DID THE CROWS PLANT CITRUS CENTER?

Just as Mr. Fogg raised the majestic Palmdale Hotel from the swamp as a place for potential buyers to stay when they set foot off the Florida East Coast Railway, another entrepreneur, Otto Wagner of the Chicago Land and Development Company, set his site on developing another area along State Road 78. Wagner's dream was even more elaborate. He envisioned a hunting club and hotel to attract the hoity-toity European adventurer. However, to appeal to those who had never experienced the Everglades, he didn't think the image of rattlesnakes, alligators, bears, and a sticky 90 percent humidity would be a very strong selling point. Otto Wagner needed a name for his dream township.

How the township got its fabled name, "Citrus Center" is linked to several difficult to prove stories. It is said that two boys, the Parker Brothers stumbled upon the small budding roadside settlement and decided to stay. When the boys planted a few citrus trees around the area, the locals began to call their blossoming homestead, Citrus Center. However, there are some discrepancies to this story, as other locals say the town got its official name from the McAllisters', the family who experimented with creating various citrus by-products to sell to passersby. Yet, another more fascinating tale is that Citrus Center was named after crow behavior. It is said that large flocks of brooding black crows would arrive every night to roost in the bushy tops of the many citrus trees. The crows apparently enjoyed the fruity citrus, discarding the seedlings into the ground. It is said that the crows sprouted the first citrus groves and gave the town its name!

A CROOK IN THE ROAD

1917—The Majestic Citrus Center Hotel

The Citrus Center Hotel constructed in 1917 was the heartbeat of Wagner's dream to attract people from Europe and the United States to the prospects of the budding town during Florida's 1900's land boom. The fabulous hotel even had electricity and running water, a real attraction for a wilderness site during those early days. As a result of a major international advertising campaign, several German families arrived from Europe including the Porterloefs', and Bernbhardts'; the Poeterloefs' managed the Hotel.

The Henry Randalls', Peeples' neighbors raised honeybees. The beeswax was used during World War One to pack and ship guns to U.S. and Allied Forces in the European and Pacific theatres. They also collected the thick sap from pine trees dripped into clay cups, to make turpentine. In the old days, turpentine was used on burns and for other medicinal purposes.

Another pioneer, Ralph Wadlow also worked in the bee factory and saved up enough cash to buy land on State Road 25 (now U.S. Hwy 27). Later the site was purchased by Cecil Clemons who created one of Florida's most imaginative roadside attractions, Gatorama. Today, Patty and Allen Register run Gatorama that announces its presence to travelers on U.S. 27 with the grimacing smile of a 60-

foot razor toothed alligator starring across the prairie from a roadside billboard. Gatorama is one of the foremost businesses in Florida on the cutting edge of a promising new economic source for Glades County: Aquaculture and Eco-tourism.

LIFE ON THE PRAIRIE

At the Citrus Center homestead, Donald Peeples, his brothers and sisters grew up in a world that required them to create their own entertainment. The kids invented games and transformed the rich resources of the natural setting into grand imaginary objects. Apart from the Field Days they looked forward to attending on the Brighton Indian Reservation, the kids burrowed long, dug out tunnels in the soft muck and made up their own games. Donald and Billy used old oilcans or wooden barrels to create a model of the familiar Florida Eastcoast Railway train that hooted its whistle stop along the tracks from Lake Placid, to Palmdale to Ortona carrying a motley crew of passengers and cypress logs to their destinations on a southern route to Immokalee, Sunnyland and Everglades City. Even buggy old cabbage palm stalks took on a life of their own providing the kids with hours of fun frolicking across the wide-open range, a freedom of spirit that children today may not understand as "fun," or are fortunate to have the space to experience. The Brighton Indian Reservation Field Days provided the area kids with an escape from everyday chores. Like all children, they raced in old corn sacks and competed in numerous events providing a break from the hard life of a working cattle ranch in the rugged terrain of Citrus Center.

The women married to cattlemen were in charge of the household as well as other duties. Donald's mother slopped through all kinds of weather, rattlesnake infested palmettos, moccasins lurking in vegetation to the cookhouse to prepare a sunrise breakfast before the cowhands hit the trail. Donald says his mother never owned any dogs, as snakes would crawl into any swollen crevice and wait to prey upon a sleepy hound looking for a cool spot to escape from the oppressive heat.

The day began early for the cow hunters. They would eat breakfast, saddle up, and wait for daylight to begin their ride to Venus on the cattle drive from Citrus Center. Often the drives stretched into eighteen-hour days with cow hunters herding steers as the moon rose high in the sky.

WASH MORGAN—CHUCKWAGON COOK

1900's—Wash Morgan, chuck wagon cook, stoked the fires on the long
"Cracker Trail" cattle drives across Central Florida

Another long revered staple of the cow hunter crew was the cornerstone of survival: the chuck wagon cook. In advance of the cattle roundup and a long day roping strays in sawgrass hutches, the familiar imprint of Wash Morgan's chuck wagon stew wafted across the prairie, leading tired cattle drivers home to the cow camp. Morgan worked for Buck King and was a hard riding, tougher than nails chuck wagon cook. Morgan's covered buckboard, pulled by the strength of long horn steers was a welcome sight to cow hunters who were weary, hungry and tired at the end of a long 20 hour cattle-driving day. The cowboys were at home on the range with a hot brew of ground coffee cradled in the grip of toughened, callused hands, looking forward to Wash Morgan's home cooking. The aroma of "Smith's Stew" (a concoction of beef innards) thickened the air on a trail of sparkling embers, melting into a canopy of stars hanging from the pitch-black night.

As the whippoorwills nestled in the hollows of cabbage palm fans the night lingered, the cowboys bedded down on saddles and crumpled blankets in makeshift lean-tos. A crisp layer of dew deposited glistening droplets into the gullies of cow horses' sloping backs. The cur dogs gave out their last contented howls and curled up nearby. The camp was laid to rest, enveloped by the grand silence and magnificence of unspoiled Nature awaiting the new light of the morning sun to start the cycle over again on their drive deep into the heart of the Everglades.

Although the notion of the *Home on the Range* cowboy as romanticized in Louis Lamoure's dime novels and the movies distance the toil and hardship of cowboy life, their lives are an inspiration to the resiliency of the human spirit and man's lust for adventure.

Today, the vision of the cowhands and Wash Morgan's ghostly chuck wagon creaking and clamoring its pots and pans, whip cracking the cattle through the gully-washed rutted trail is a legend that can almost be heard in the whisper of the wind on the now overgrown passages of the Glades County cowboy cracker trails.

FROM BOOM TO BUST

During the 1930s, continual cycles of prosperity and economic crisis loomed over Citrus Center still a "hope" in the hearts of people who settled there. Donald Peeples mother persistently pursued every means to hold the community together. Ma Peeples traded some of their land for a paved road into the town. With the area underwater most of the time, Mrs. Peeples negotiated a ten acre trade with the prison camp at nearby Edge for labor and construction of the road. Until the paved roadway was built, the old Model T's and wagons dug their graves in the thick, black muck wherever they broke down.

However, not even the newly paved road could save Citrus Center from its doom; Citrus City and the Chicago Land Development Company eventually became a victim of the tough Depression. The town went bust and just plain, "shut down." However, the staunch Will of a few families secured their survival and sank their roots deeper into Citrus Center.

Donald and Dorothy Peeples still reside at their ranch on State Road 78 where there was once a town. Their homestead is surrounded by a clutch of oak and cabbage palms next to the wooden stalls housing Donald's cow horses. Even the feisty Bay horse that got spooked and threw an experienced cowboy, Donald Peeples to the ground breaking his shoulder, innocently peers from the stall. These cow horses seem to possess an awareness of another set of life's rules; they are part of the cowboy lore and history, they are the other part of a team that gave birth to the cattle industry.

Donald and Dorothy Peeples speak of the cowboy legends with down-to-earth warmth. They open their albums and talk the stories as a remembrance from their own past. However, down the long curving entrance to the road that Donald's mother traded land for "pavement," there is no evidence of a monument to Citrus Center, or the pioneers who carved a niche in Glades County's history.

What remains today of the graceful splendor of Citrus Center Hotel, the church, the post office, the warehouse (where victims of the 1926 hurricane were housed), the schoolhouse, the bee house and store is a lone street sign and two cement foundations across from the Peeples' homestead.

Two cement foundations mark the remains of the 1900's "Boom town"—Citrus Center

Like Mr. Fogg's "Garden of Eden" vision of the Palmdale Land Company and most of the people who followed their dreams to Mr. Wagner's Citrus Center are buried in the forever-silent secrets taken back by the Everglades. The one time beauty of the classic Citrus Center Hotel where sportsman showed off their day's hunting trophies is long gone. The Depression took its toll on land and people but it gave the early pioneers something unexpected, probably not appreciated during hard times; it gave them a sense of becoming part of the land, learning how to nurture it so in turn, it would give life to their families.

However, there is something far more valuable than the tombstone of a ghost town. What is very much alive today are the stories that leap from the sepia album pictures freeze-framed in time of those who contributed to Glades County's history. Who would have known that these old pictures capturing hard working people just going about their daily tasks would one day commemorate the vanished life of Citrus Center? The stories are retold again and again as a tribute to a cultural heritage and history of Glades County's cow hunters. The Peeples' family has earned their unique place in Florida's pioneer history.

5

WHERE THE SWALLOWTAIL KITE SOARS

◆

GLADES COUNTY

D.R. Kilpatrick, grandson and wife, Dannie

When D. R. Kilpatrick rode the open ranges across Florida, it was characterized by the romanticism of cowboy folklore. In the old days, cattle left by the Spanish from the 1500s were free for the taking; the stock from which the Florida cattle industry was bred. When Kilpatrick talks about Florida's unique cow hunter legacies, it's like sitting by a campfire visualizing a vanishing history that can hardly be imagined.

The picture unfolds with cow hunters and their cur dogs cutting trails through dense virgin swamps across Central Florida. Confronted by wild cats, boars and insects, they captured, branded, bred and drove the cattle herds to market on the east and west coasts of Florida. During summer drives, long steamy days melted into sweltering, humid nights when lightening tore from dark forces releasing torrential rains, soaking the dry soil into a quicksand of muck. Cow hunters bedded down in the merest palmetto clumps shared with other creeping creatures of the night searching for a place to dodge pellets of hail and wind. The cattle huddled together in tightly knit furry bundles, as if their shear numbers could protect them from the assault of the drenching downpour and black clouds of mosquitoes.

In the 1930's, D. R. Kilpatrick drove cattle north from Moore Haven, at the bottom of Lake Okeechobee, to Fort Pierce on the east coast. "In those days, before fences and dykes changed the structure of the land and natural flow of water," Kilpatrick said, "we herded cattle all the way across Central Florida, meandering through the prairie, letting cattle graze along the way. We stopped along the trail a couple of times to brand cows and steers, then sold them the rest of the time, it don't bother."

As sunset shadows merged into ink black nights, the chuck wagon cook stoked his fires, curling the smell of potatoes and biscuits high into the sky, announcing to hearty appetites along the trail that a reward waited at the end of a hard days work, washed down with a tin of pan boiled coffee.

Eventually, cowboys settled on large sprawling ranches and began to improve breeding practices. From the scrawny scrub cattle, pioneer cattle growers learned how to breed a hearty stock that could survive the harsh Everglades climate. With fortitude and will, the staunch pioneers who settled in Glades, Okeechobee and Highlands counties were the forefathers of the State's cattle industry.

THE "CRACKER TRAIL"

D. R. and Dannie, married 53 years on June 15th, 1999 courted across Florida's coast-to-coast "cracker trail." Kilpatrick met Dannie after one long cattle drive across the Lake to the market in Ft. Pierce. A whirlwind of dusty, clattering hooves and horns announced Kilpatrick's arrival as he drove the herd into what he described as "the one horse town of Ft. Pierce," up Delaware Avenue to the front door of the Ideal Holding Company. It was here that a young lady named Dannie, who helped him restock supplies, caught his eye. After a brief time, D. R. took Dannie to be his "cowgirl" and lifelong partner who continued to help him build their thriving agribusiness in the middle of the Moore Haven prairie. They lived a folklore lifestyle that future generations will never know except in books that preserve those memories forever. Sitting across a dining room table from D. R. and Dannie with a fresh brew of coffee, carries the imagination back to those times, on a dream and a wish. This living history becomes one with those who stop to listen, learn and pass along the stories that will never occur again in this lifetime.

D. R. Kilpatrick's father and family trickled down to the Lake from St. Augustine during the Second Seminole War (1835–42). During the Civil War, his Great Granddaddy drove cattle across the Caloosahatchee River into Punta Rassa (near Ft. Myers) where paddle wheeled boats carried them to Cuba. After the Spanish American War, cattle were depleted in Cuba; thus, South Florida cattlemen replenished the stock and traded for supplies. Kilpatrick said that "paddle boat Captain James McKay snuck through the maze of Ten Thousand Islands at the tip of the peninsula in the dark of night to run the Union blockade as the soldiers had stopped all shipments to and from the Confederate States." Captain McKay developed what is called the "cow cavalry" headed up by C. J. Munnerlyn and other cattlemen such as Howell T. Lykes that pioneered the early cattle trade between Florida and Cuba.

As the cattle industry evolved, hand made fences were erected to cordon off land, but change did not occur very rapidly. D.R. said there "just weren't too many hearty takers for the job of cow hunter." Yet, in the early days, family operated cattle growers had greater control over their business than today. Each piece of property "had to be understood with a natural common sense not learned from a book but being raised up from the roots in the business." Water and grazing land was plentiful but difficult seasonal changes and infestation of cattle diseases were the major difficulties cattle growers faced. When there was drought, the cowboys waited, improvised, eventually the rains came in torrents, the pastures replenished with carpets of green, and then the cycle began again.

In the 1900's, Kilpatrick remembers the gradual changes from cattle marketing to the early stages of tourism. New hotels and townships began to sprout up in the middle of nowhere; some lasted a few years, while others returned to dust in the wind. Hopeful business ventures of Northern entrepreneurs disappeared, as the Everglades relentlessly absorbed their dreams. The cattle industry pioneers planted their roots deeper, surviving drought, floods and fires, establishing their heritage in Glades County. Today, many of the cow hunter descendants still work the land of their forefathers and carry on the legacy of the Florida cattle industry. However, many of the younger generation have also left and let go of their heritage for jobs in the city or for lack of financial resources to pay large inheritance taxes on the land.

Kilpatrick's concern for the cattle industry was not only about the present but the future. He said that circumstances in the cattle industry are different today. Recent changes in the way cattle grow out and what they are fed affect the business. There is a decline in the cattle industry. Importation of grass-fattened cattle has had the greatest effect on the market. Frozen meat from Australia and New Zealand put slaughterhouses out of business in Miami, Jacksonville and Tampa. New technology now puts more frozen foreign meat in supermarkets (although fruits/vegetables are required to be labeled as to country of origin, beef remains anonymous as to country of origin). As a member of The National Cattlemen's and Beef Association, Kilpatrick was one of the leaders who took the issue to Washington in support of labeling foreign beef.

The labeling of beef origin was of major importance when bovine spongiform encephalopathy (BSE) or "mad cow" disease surfaced in 1986 in Germany, Great Britain, Belgium, France and Canada. The handling of "mad cow" disease caused government heads to roll in Europe, when the break out was attributed to imported United Kingdom beef containing ground sheep parts infected with "scrapie" added into cattle feed (scrapie, a disease found in sheep, similar to BSE in cattle, contaminates cow feed and causes BSE in cattle). Because the UK doesn't have as much cropland, animal-based proteins were commonly fed to cattle.

According to the Canadian Cattlemen's Association, sheep diagnosed with scrapie were incinerated or buried and are never allowed to go to abattoirs, renderers or enter cattle feed.

In 2003, after many years of strict regulations on U.S. beef producers, maintaining a clean slate from "mad cow" disease was marred; BSE appeared in the United States imported from a Canadian dairy herd. The scare came five years after Charles D. Lambert, Chief Economist of the National Cattleman's Beef

Association testified before the Subcommittee on Trade of the House Committee on Ways and Means in 1999, "livestock producers are becoming increasingly dependant on the rest of the world to buy our products. Exports of meat and grains make sense for the U. S. that has only four percent of the world's population, but a large share of the world's agricultural production. Exports of beef have helped to take up the slack of a declining demand for beef at home."

In December 2003, when mad cow disease was discovered in the dairy cow imported from Canada to Washington State, the export of beef came to a sudden halt. Even though more stringent standards on U. S. beef production were initiated by the United States Department of Agriculture, it was too late for the consummation of an historical trade deal negotiated between three Florida cattle growers and Cuba.

During the period that the mad cow disease controversy was at its height, three Florida cattle growers had consummated an $8 million dollar deal to re-establish agricultural trade with Cuba that Kilpatrick indicated began in the Civil War era. Parke Wright, of the J.P. Wright Company long time cattle grower from Naples, Florida (related to the Lykes Brothers family of cattle growers in Glades County) brokered the first cattle deal in forty-years with the Cuban government. Alimports, a Cuban government controlled company, agreed to purchase 500 head of Florida cattle to rebuild their beef industry. Since the U.S. Cuban embargo, the population of eleven million people has been short on milk and meat. The Cuban/U.S. beef deal was made possible as part of President Bill Clinton's 2000 legislation relaxing the Cuban embargo for humanitarian exports including grain, citrus, dairy and cattle. The agreement was solidified in September 2002, when U.S. producers participated in Cuba's first international trade exposition. At the close of the historic meeting, millions of dollars worth of agricultural products from across the U.S. were negotiated for Cuban exportation.

In March of 2004, the Florida cattle were to be shipped to Port Mariel, Cuba, however, Alimport's representative Jose Alvarez, feared the possible exportation of "mad cow" disease to Cuba, thus, the deal was postponed indefinitely.

CHANGES IN BEEF PRODUCTION: FATTENING THE CALVES AT THE FEEDLOTS

"The appearance of feedlots and feedlot cattle also had its effect on the early cattle business," Kilpatrick said. "It changed the type of meat people consumed. There used to be a lot more veal (fattened calves) and now calves are sold to 'feeders' a lot thinner at a discounted price. New processes have been introduced that require the thinner calf to be fattened up at the feeder, cutting profits for cattle growers. Then there is the issue of bad publicity on the health of beef (before the BSE scare). This bad publicity did not occur before feedlots were introduced in the business as places where cows are fattened as the last stage before slaughter. In the early days, part of the slaughterhouse practice was to hang beef after slaughter to improve taste. Now this final stage has been eliminated. The American public more than likely doesn't know anymore what it's like to taste a good piece of beef."

NOT ENOUGH WATER FOR 1,000 NEW PEOPLE A DAY

But there are other changes altering Florida that will never turn back the pages of history: The ability of water and land to sustain a healthy condition with the population explosion, and urban expansion threatening to squeeze agribusiness out of the State. "The population on the coasts is so great," said Kilpatrick, "that harming Lake Okeechobee cannot be avoided" (seventy-percent of Florida's population live on the coasts). Lake Okeechobee is the prime water supply for agribusiness in surrounding counties, as well as the major water supply for urban areas and the Everglades.

What does Kilpatrick perceive as a solution for agribusiness to survive with enough water for pastures, citrus, cane and vegetables competing with urban development? He said there is enough water wasted in Florida to take care of the future. Although the environmentalists may oppose such a move, if a pipeline were constructed out of Wakulla Springs, Silver Springs, Weekeewachee and the Crystal River, (all natural spring water), and it could flow to urban areas, there would be enough water to serve South Florida. Another possible solution: Capitalizing on Florida as a peninsula surrounded by salt water. Desalinization dates back to World War II when salt water was filtered to make fresh water aboard ships at sea. The cost of this advanced technology may be well worth the expenditure to save agribusiness and supply additional water to urban areas. Presently, agriculture recycles water back to the Lake, but big wells for urban use reduce the aquifer and lower it. Creature comfort services like car washes, golf courses, sewers and other perks of city life all take its toll on the Lake and the State. Agricultural experts are of the opinion that Florida's natural resources cannot support a completely urbanized state.

KEEPING THE LAND ALIVE

D. R. Kilpatrick, according to Okeechobee Livestock Market manager/owner Pete Clemens, knew the Land and Lake Okeechobee better than anyone. Besides his concern for the future of the cattle industry, he was concerned about the health of the Lake and water control by the South Florida Water Management District (SFWMD).

The decision to raise or lower water levels in Lake Okeechobee affects the livelihood of agribusinesses (cattle/cane/citrus/vegetables); the SFWMD makes these decisions determined by a Board that sets policy and direction for the Agency. Nine individuals, each representing specific geographic areas within the District are appointed to the Board by the Governor and confirmed by the Florida Senate. The members serve, without pay, generally for a four-year term. There is a staff of about 1, 650 employees to carry out the Board's directives. Under Florida Statute, Chapter 373, the SFWMD is authorized to adopt rules and regulations for which it is specifically granted authority.

The District's rules encompass Right of Way management; environmental resource, consumptive use, and right of way occupancy permitting; public access, use and enjoyment of District-owned lands; real property acquisition and disposal; procedures for contracting of professional and contractual services (including supplier diversity and outreach contract, and bid protest procedures). The decisions made by the Board regarding water apportionment and water quality in Lake Okeechobee, according to Kilpatrick, are crucial to the survival of agribusiness in the Florida. Kilpatrick's "grass roots" opinion is emphatic regarding the fate of the Lake and reciprocally, the cattle industry due to increased regulations on water quality and usage. Kilpatrick believes that "the last nail driven in the coffin of Lake Okeechobee was in 1970 when new regulations prevented cattle from grazing the Lake bottom. Cattle used to keep torpedo grass and willows eaten back. One cow eats 40 to 50 pounds of grass a day. After the cattle were prohibited from the Lake, not much could be done to bring back the Lake very fast."

D. R. Kilpatrick, born in Okeechobee County in 1920, worked cattle with his father before Congress voted in 1947 to build a levy around the Lake to protect low lying areas and burgeoning towns such as Moore Haven from disasters like the 1926 and 28 hurricanes. "The days before the levy, muck around the Lake used to be sometimes as high as a house. Muck used to accumulate in the bottom of Lake Okeechobee and the natural wave action took water to the edge where it would accumulate then dry back away," Kilpatrick said. "In those days, most of the outlying land from the Lake was marsh, matter of fact, where Port LaBelle golf course is on Highway 80 on the Calhoosahatchee River, there used to be a waterfall in the river on the west side of Lake Flirt (the early Indians mention canoeing to Lake Flirt that today no longer exists; it's a "dead river"). Before various levies were built on the Caloosahatchee River to artificially control water, there were natural rock formations or blockages that affected the inflow and out-flow of water.

CARVING UP FLORIDA

In Florida's 1920's boom days, new settlers discovered the beauty of the land and its natural waterways with people arriving by boat, train and on makeshift roads. Eventually, manmade canals were carved across land through the Lake for boat travel across the state and for drainage. The Hillsborough Canal at Ft Lauderdale was mainly constructed for boat traffic and the St. Lucie Canal constructed for both purposes. Cross-state canals cut off 400 miles of boat travel by going through Lake Okeechobee. In the 1960's, artificial control of water on the Kississmee River leading to Fisheating Creek came with the building of a levy. Although water regulation used to be under the Flood Control District and the Corps of Engineers, today the South Florida Water Management District manages water quality, control and monitoring.

As a pioneer cattleman and cane grower, D. R. Kilpatrick was concerned about restrictions placed on agribusiness for water usage. "I don't think anything in the world can be done to improve the quality of the Lake. Several years back when grass was disappearing in the Lake, the SFWMD released grass tarp in Lake Okeechobee that was supposed to be 97% sterile to eat out hydralla. The tarp is not native to the Lake. The three percent of the tarp that were not sterile did reproduce, destroying the breeding grass for fish." Kilpatrick believed that agriculture was being driven out of Florida due to water restrictions, a similar view expressed by Pete Clemons longtime cattle/citrus grower and owner of the Okeechobee Livestock Market, as well as Stanlo Johns, long time cattle manager for the Brighton Seminole Reservation.

THE CATTLE BUSINESS FORECAST

Kilpatrick said with facetious humor "that if agribusiness is driven out of the State, people will have to get all their food from the supermarket." In Florida, agribusiness creates $62 billion to the State's economy; it's the number two industry with tourism ranked number one, and construction, number three. According to the Economic Research Service, the USDA reports receipts from Florida agricultural product in 1999 amounting to $7.07 billion. This is a 1.5 increase from the previous year. Cash receipts from all crops increased 2.3 percent from 1998, and cash receipts from all livestock and livestock products decreased by only 1.9 percent. All cattle and calves on Florida farms and ranches as of January 1, 1999 totaled 1, 800,000 head down 4 percent from 1998, and 8 percent below January 1, 1997. Calves born during 1998 totaled 950,000 head, 3 percent below 1997, and 7 percent below 1996. All cattle and calves in the United States as of January 1, 2000 totaled 98.0 million head, 1 percent below the 99.1 million of Jan. 1997. The total economic impact on Florida from agribusinesses from farm to supermarket is approximately $45 billion.

The cattle industry in Florida represents a continual income stream to agribusiness and is a major economic factor in Glades, Okeechobee and Highlands Counties. But the cattle industry is also a highly volatile agri-product as it depends on uncontrollable and unpredictable factors of market price and weather condition to determine market share. Although Florida ranks mid-range below large cattle producing states such as Texas, South Dakota, Nebraska, the cattle industry is a big business in the United States.

Over time, beef standards have become more technologically driven with the introduction of feedlots for grow out with the United States Department of Agriculture (USDA) regulating cattle growers. With new international pressures on the cattle industry such as NAFTA and GATT, these may be significant but not a crucial threat to the domestic market. In a 1999 address to the Florida Cattlemen's Association, Jim Handley Executive Vice President said that it is important to "take care of our domestic market. The overwhelming majority of U. S. consumers, we believe, will buy and purchase U. S. grown beef, it's the safest in the world."

As agribusiness diversifies and land is converted to accommodate urban development in Florida, threatening Glades County's cattle growers, one Arcadia rancher sums it up in this way: "In the early days, people in agriculture ran the politics of this nation. While these individuals developed their own independent lifestyle, they furnished the urbanite with the best and least expensive food in the world. Now natural resources are managed. Today, we are being pushed from every side. The environmentalists challenge our right to be where we are, the animal rights activists challenge our ways of doing things, and the bureaucracies complicate our doing anything. But to accomplish self-preservation, we must have progress through change."

These words echo Glades County pioneer, D.R. Kilpatrick who predicted in 1930 that "progress" would eventually threaten the local cattle industry. For the pioneer cattlemen and women, the wind and water twisted the land and molded the people in the "school of hard knocks," learning how to resonate with the Land and support their survival. Only down the road into the Future will one know if intervening "manmade" projects can return the already carved up and altered land to its former design by Mother Nature.

EVERGLADES RESTORATION

As Florida became a magnet for tourists attracted to the sun, surf and wide-open spaces, urbanization began to enclose on the central corridors of land. New laws were enacted on land and water usage that brought manmade controls on irrigation and flood control. Today, Florida is carved up in all directions, and the natural sustaining resources of the Land are suffocating. Thus, in 1983 a "Save the Everglades" project was initiated by then Florida Governor Bob Graham to restore the "natural health of this precious ecosystem." The Everglades Restoration Act of 2000 calls for "pilot projects to restore the natural flow of water and improve water-related needs to the region." However, despite all of the publicity on the restoration effort, D. R. Kilpatrick said that the eight billion dollar Everglades Restoration Act "will never return the land to the way it was." Perhaps those that served the land and that the land served before it was changed, envision the project as a "pipedream."

The Environmentalists say that the $8 billion dollar Everglades Restoration Act planned over 30 years will "restore" the natural flow of water through a number of construction projects. Some of the plans include: the construction of deep wells to pump water into the Florida aquifer; a study of seepage in water preserve areas and waste water treatment; a study of ground reservoir technology and a proposed $204 million for water storage and treatment plant in Okeechobee County.

According to Florida Trend Magazine, there are approximately 5,000 people a week moving into Florida; it is one of the fastest growing states in the USA. Florida accounts for one in every ten new jobs produced in the United States. Florida's labor force of 7.3 million ranks as the nation's fourth largest. According to the 2000 census, it is anticipated that Florida is moving up the ladder from its ranking as the fourth most populated state in the Union. (California ranks #1, New York #2 and Texas #3).

From D. R. Kilpatrick's historical perspective, the Restoration Project "will not return Florida to its natural state when Florida was a territory in 1823, before it became a State in 1845. The only way this might possibly happen, is if they moved everybody out that didn't have roots here at that time. They can stay."

Pioneer cow-hunter, D. R. Kilpatrick, passed on in 2000.

Photo: *Courtesy of Bud Adams, The Adams Ranch, Ft. Pierce, Florida*

6

"TRUE COW HUNTERS WEAR STETSON'S," VANCE WHIDDEN

✦

MOORE HAVEN

Vance Whidden
1999

The year was 1919, when Glades cow hunter Vance Whidden was born. It was also the date that the first global war was officially called: "The Great War," (later called World War I) that left Old Europe in an aftermath of rubble destroying many historical landmarks and setting a precedent for numbering world conflicts. None of these "Great Wars" ever ended up on American soil although many American lives were sacrificed.

The only war fought on American soil was the Civil War; it pitted American against American, dividing families and loyalty. However, Rebel Captain John Wesley Whidden (Vance Whidden's grandfather) and his brother, a Captain in the Union army, managed to heal the wounds of War and were re-united without holding grudges. Captain Whidden began the family tradition as a Glades County cow hunter when he started a cattle business during the Civil War years.

Born in Arcadia on April 15, Vance Whidden conveys a strong image of the Glades cow hunter sitting tall in the saddle, even as he relaxes in a folding chair in the park amidst a crowd of those returning for the annual Moore Haven reunion. "Don't make me out to be a hero, I'm not," gently prods Vance Whidden in an unassuming manner. He does not acknowledge the fact that he is a "living legend" representing a long line of Glades County heroes: The cow hunters. These young cowboys carved a lifestyle from the natural resources of the wilderness, built a business, raised families and survived on their original wit and ingenuity. It's easy to honor the lives of these Glades pioneers.

The Whidden family was involved in many young business opportunities that sprung up around Lake Okeechobee in the 1800–1900's. Vance Whidden remembers traveling through the woods across Big Bear Beach with horse and wagon to deliver mail on his father's route from Lakeport to Palmdale. Like everything else, supplies moved by horse, rail, or boat on what Mr. Whidden calls "washboard roads" from Lake Okeechobee to Elderberry near Indian Prairie Canal.

Vance Whidden's dad worked for the Atlantic Seaboard Railroad setting tracks when the railroad first connected Arcadia southward, boosting commerce development along the way. Whidden's cousins were commercial fishermen on the Lake near Lakeport about 20 miles from where Vance Whidden grew up. However, cattle and hogs provided the basic income for the Whidden family.

1926 HURRICANE

It was 1926 when seven year old Vance Whidden and the family were living in the woods near Lakeport, nature unleashed upon the "people of the Lake," one of the worst disasters in Florida history. Torrential rains blew horizontal arrows through the wind ripping up trees by the root, leveling everything in its wake. A ground swell of water rose like a tidal wave sweeping through the Whidden house from early afternoon until the next day. Vance recalls "water moccasins floating through the house, but they didn't hurt anybody, they just wanted to get to higher ground." The family of five sisters and a brother, and the Moore Haven school teacher, managed to escape the flood at Norton's "pole house." While the group waited out the storm, Mr. Norton hauled out a one hundred pound sack of rice and flour to make syrup and biscuits. When the blow subsided, the Whiddens' struggled home by wagon to check on the devastation. When they arrived, they sadly discovered that everything was destroyed except for one sign of life. A clever hog had managed to ride out the storm by his own methods. Vance Whidden said that a 60-foot cypress tree had blown down and was floating on its side. On top of the tree, there sat a big old hog, the last one left from a cattle trade of short horned Devon Cattle just before the storm. As it turned out, the pig saved the lives of the Norton refugees. Whidden returned to the pole house with the prize pig and they enjoyed the luxury of barbecued pork to go along with the other vittles served during the three week stay at the pole house.

As the water subsided and the townspeople came from their make-do shelters, there was little left that looked familiar. The hurricane spilled an avalanche of water from Lake Okeechobee over all of the low-lying areas, destroying lives and the little town of Moore Haven that rested at the foot of the big Lake.

After the '26 hurricane, picking of the pieces was quickened with the help of the American Legion, the Red Cross and volunteers; the indomitable spirit of the people of Moore Haven could not be defeated. Life finally returned to some normalcy, the hog and cattle drives resumed as young Vance Whidden helped his dad "get 500 head of hogs, herded like sheep, to Port Charlotte where they were bought and sold by Luther Coon and shipped off to Cuba. The pigs were weighed on a cotton scale, as they were tied by the legs and hung down to touch the scale with notches that determined their weight. The pigs brought four cents weight'."

PATROLING THE COASTLINE

When World War II broke out, Vance Whidden, at 22, joined the United States Coast Guard. He was sent to Key West for submarine patrols along the Florida Keys to Martinique. By this time, Whidden had tied the knot with a long time childhood friend, Abbie Williams. The two married in Okeechobee in 1942, celebrating 58 years of marriage on September 25th, 1999.

In the Navy, Vance Whidden's unique cow hunter skills were in demand. His ability to splice anything together in any type of configuration and circumstance earned Whidden a quick rise to Boatswain's Mate, besides the fact that he received a 3.99 of 4.0 on the written test. "During the war, the Navy was short of officers so one could rise to the command of a patrol boat in a short amount of time if he could pass the tests." However, Whidden said there was one officer with a "sleeve of harsh marks" who did not believe that Whidden could have scored so high on the Boatswain Mate's test, when most sailors failed. The Captain himself decided to re-test Whidden. When the results produced the same high score again for Whidden, it won him a promotion to Boatswain Mate Second Class awarded to him by the noted "hash marked" Commanding Officer.

Whidden spent the war years on Navy patrol duty, checking merchant ships anchored at the continental limit for any possible stowed enemy supplies or enemies. The cow hunter's agility to "cut cows" came in handy in cutting off vessels spotted by the Navy patrol and maneuvering them into port. With the fine-tuned hands of a cow hunter steering his cutting horse through unruly steers, Whidden led his men through many encounters with renegade vessels. He used his finely honed ingenuity, wit and strategy to safely guide his patrol boat through pitch black nights, hedging along jagged coral reefs, veering through invisible mine fields. Whidden and his crew spent tireless double shifts halting vessels, putting a Navy man on board, and manipulating vessels through the offshore Navy defense radar barriers.

Traveling from Miami to the Keys, patrol boats could be seen protecting Florida's slender shoreline from German and Japanese submarines stealthily cruising underwater near the Miami Shelf. Whidden says there were many "sleepless, nights chasing subs, having to be alert to decipher Morse code signals from the 'wind guns' posted on shore battery." He recalls one frightening incident when a merchant ship tried to run. "The Commanding Officer called for help. I pulled out the bullhorn and ordered the vessel to turn about, instead the vessel opened fire. I had to run across in front of the boat to get it to stop so I could put some-one on to get a manifest; I shot off a 20-millimeter. This time he stopped, turned around and I put someone on board to ride the boat in," described Whidden.

As a Navy man, Whidden also served in Nova Scotia and Maryland where he went to "fire school" in the Panama Canal. He even pursued two Japanese sub-marines in the Bering Straits of Alaska, "the roughest water I have ever seen!" However, despite his tough resiliency, it was the mosquitoes that got the best of him. Whidden contracted malaria while in Panama that put him in a San Fran-cisco hospital. After a couple of bouts with the disease, he was assigned to the Richmond, California base where "we loaded ammo at Port Chicago. The job was dangerous. No match, no lighter or friction was allowed that might cause the base to accidentally blow up." During the night shift, Whidden says, "loading ammunition onto the ship, meant posting men to stand behind each person haul-ing the boxes on deck to be sure no sparks were ignited." A spark could detonate tons of live explosives!

BACK ON THE RANGE

When Whidden finished his tour of duty with the Navy in 1946, he returned to his life as a cow hunter in Glades County. By now the likes of chuck wagon cook, Wash Morgan who used steers to advance the cow hunters' campsite had been replaced by Model T's. While Whidden was away from home, "the horses got grown and I had to train them. A horse called Prince was one of the most intelli-gent that I ever had. I hate to this day that I sold him. He was part Texas Mus-tang and Quarter Horse. His mouth was so sensitive that you could handle him with two fingers." Vance Whidden adjusts his Stetson, as if in an unconscious "salute" to the memory of his not forgotten cow horse.

Whidden worked for Lykes brothers, and also helped Donald Peeples when he needed it at nearby Citrus Center. "Everyone helped out each other. Donald Pee-ples was a good neighbor."

Vance Whidden's life is a tribute to the growth of Florida's cattle industry in Glades County. Vance Whidden was Mayor of Moore Haven four times and on the Glades County Commission for twenty years.

But, there are few "trade secrets" Vance Whidden reveals for those would not rec-ognize the subtle "tip off" of a true cow hunter. It is how the cow hunter wears the Stetson. "A beginner wears the hat not shaped round. To be a real cowboy the men wear the hat to the side, like mine. You're darn right I'm a cowboy! It's been said before: Ready for a fight or a girlfriend, whichever one comes first. It's a great life, but you can starve to death doing it!"

Vance Whidden's life is a reminder that the cow hunter lore is not just a collection of make-believe stories told to generation after generation around a campfire. In Glades County, the cow hunters are a living legend of courage, character, strength and a tribute to Florida history.

Pioneer cow hunter Vance Whidden passed away in 2001.

7

"WE ARE THE ENEMY AND THE ENEMY IS US"

KING OF THE CATTLE AUCTION: PETE CLEMONS

A cloud of dust hazes the afternoon sun kicked up by steel barreled cattle carriers and their load of motley colored cows herding into a narrow wooden tunnel to the underground guts of the Okeechobee Livestock Market. Guttural baritone moos, and hooves stomping on hardwood, resonate to the 30 year practiced chant of Livestock Auctioneer Wendell Cooper, seated stately in his well-worn recliner as he responds to almost indiscernible signals for bids from studied buyers bleachered on the sidelines. The livestock auction this day is busy, as cattlemen rush their stock to market before drought conditions result in catastrophic losses. The livestock market is the "bottom line" for cattle growers in Glades and surrounding counties. This is where the buck stops, where the cattle and calves are sent West mainly to Texas and Oklahoma for grazing and fattening, then to the feedlot, where they are slaughtered, packaged and returned as beefsteaks and hamburger. It is here that Pete Clemons, rodeo rider, horse racer for Joe Peeples, Sr., Animal Husbandry graduate from the University of Florida, World War II Vet born in Kissimmee, Florida began the family business in June, 1961 when his father, Q. J. Hazellief and he purchased the market instituted by the Okeechobee County Cattlemen's Association in 1939.

The phone rings continuously in Pete Clemons' office as he fields questions and responds with predictions about the Lake Okeechobee water level, when the drought might end, and the possibility of government supplements for feed and cattle losses. According to Pete Clemons, in the fall of 2000, the South Florida Water Management District (SFWMD) in West Palm Beach (overseen by a Governor appointed Board) decided to lower Lake Okeechobee by three feet, releasing fresh water into the ocean (an additional impact on salinity in tidal estuaries). Due to the lower water level in the Lake and the lack of rain, a water shortage crisis occurred. In analyzing the state of affairs, Pete Clemons explained, "In November, the Lake was approximately eleven feet (five feet below last year's level of sixteen feet). The best maintenance level of the Lake for irrigation of pastures is between twelve to fourteen feet. In the summer, when the rains and winds blow in with low pressure, the Lake is churned up and water is flushed, cleaned and circulated. Now there are dams and water levels controlled by the SFWMD."

Pete Clemons takes a strong stand, similar to Brighton Reservation's long time Cattle Manager, Stanlo Johns regarding water restrictions imposed on cattle growers by the South Florida Water Management District that affects the livelihood of the cattle industry. "The District," says Clemons "does not consult with the people who know the Lake and understand its needs such as pioneer cattleman and cane grower D. R. Kilpatrick. The history of the SFWMD is one of very bad decisions, although they have created jobs. Even if the SFWMD is comprised of practical, knowledgeable people, they still cannot solve all of the problems that oppose one another: the Environmentalists, the Urban Developers, Agriculturists and the Politicians, that exploit it all. The headwaters of the Kissimmee River are already polluted due to the downstream flow of pollutants from the highly populated Disney area. Although Disneyworld takes pride in maintaining a healthy environment, their advanced technology cannot diminish the strain on natural resources. The natural filtration system of the ecosystem cannot instantly recycle and purify a massive onslaught of waste and pollution that filters down the river and seeps into the watershed." Experts say that Florida's natural resources cannot sustain a fully urbanized state.

"The cattle industry, however, will survive the future," although Pete Clemons emphasizes, 'it may give way to developers who have more money and political clout. But, the cattle industry will be important to South Florida for sometime despite all of the obstacles." A suggested moratorium on building and the influx of people may not be feasible with an estimated l, 000 people a day moving to Florida. Tourism is the number one generator of income in the State's economy with agri-business and construction competing for top rank. Clemons says, "the opposing forces are irresolvable unless the government buys back some of the land for conservation easements (as Florida recently did in the purchase and setting aside of more than 60,000 acres of Lykes Brothers property in Glades County for a conservation easement and Wildlife Management Area part of a three phase negotiation costing $42 million).

Also, as in other places, the State can buy back 'development rites' that restricts land use to agriculture and does not take the property off the tax roles. In this way, the government can preserve the natural land required to run a good cattle farm and still have productive land."

"The future of the cattle business," said Clemons, "hinges upon two unpredictable factors: market price and weather; two things you can't do anything about. Unlike swine and poultry, the two competing meat products, the cattle business is not automated. Poultry can be produced in thousands of tightly quartered cages in long warehouses with prescribed feeding and predictable results, like in a manufacturing process. You can't do that with cows, or at least no one has yet found a way. Cattle growers are a special breed. Big companies try to get into the cattle business to do certain things, and often can't make it." Although Peter Clemons holds an Animal Husbandry degree from the University of Florida he attended on the GI bill after the Navy and WW II, he says, "the cattle business cannot be learned from a book; it takes lots of common sense. There is no program to learn the business."

The challenge to survive in the cattle business is an every day process. Every piece of property has different assets; the cattleman has to apply a daily common sense. It is a special knowledge of nature that is learned 'hands-on,' degrees don't matter," said Clemons. "Most of the big Florida ranchers that are still around have pioneered the business and made the land fertile over time for the coming of agriculture. There is no formal education, no formula, just good judgment. But, in the past ten years, urban development keeps pressing on the land. In twenty years, I won't say that the count of those in the cattle business won't be affected. There might be 10 to 20% less cattle, but the cattle continue to grow out better and heavier with more pounds of beef. The cattle business is also affected by the cost of new regulations from overseers such as the Army Corps of Engineers, Environmental Protection Agency, the Water Management District and other governmental monitoring agencies on an industry that comprises not more than three percent of the population. It is a larger land user than citrus, and historically contributes a continual stream of income to agribusiness."

The perennial droughts and floods, a condition of Florida's subtropical climate affects all agricultural interests with each entity competing for the one number natural resource: water, either too much or too little. The political battle over Florida's limited natural resource is a battle of competing forces additionally including the sport fishing industry with a strong lobby in Tallahassee. Fisherman view lower lake levels as more conducive to fish breeding that attracts international sports fisherman and worldwide publicity to the area. In Tallahassee, "It's the squeaky wheel that gets the grease," Clemons reiterated.

When drought faces cattle growers, Pete Clemons says a solution occurs either by natural or governmental intervention. "Five years ago in March, a 'no name' storm suddenly drifted out of a low-pressure system resulting in more than ten inches of rain at one time. These things occur unexpectedly and certainly solve drought. However, by summertime when we get rain and the crisis is over, the government more than likely accesses cattle growers losses and reimburses cattle people 75–80% of the feed cost in a program sponsored by the Agricultural Soil and Conservation Service (ASCS). If a drought worsens and results in cattle death losses, the money provides for restocking, although it has not ever gotten that bad in South Florida." Pete Clemons adds that providing a level of cost reimbursement for cattle losses to maintain the breeding herds is far more practical than the $20 million dollars spent on Panther Crossings along Alligator Alley. In all of his years as a cattleman cutting trails through the marshes and prairie he has glimpsed only a very few times a panther streaking into the brush.

THE BIRTH OF THE CATTLE INDUSTRY

The cattle industry is made up of a certain type of person whose character is expressed in a quiet reserve, a dedication to family, God, and the Land that they honor as a source of Life. Probably one of the least known progressions in Florida's history is how the cattle drivers tamed and cured the land for the production of agriculture. It was the pioneer cattlemen who macheted through the entangled foliage of Everglades jungle, tramped horses, oxen and wagons through razor sharp sawgrass swamp and heat that sucked the fat from the bones. Since the 1800's, buckboards followed the herds loaded with meager staples used by creative women to cook possum, squirrel, biscuits, and whatever else the land provided to support their little families. With a tough survivalist Spirit, they bore their children on the trail and kept on going no matter what until they were able to carve a homestead from the land. It was the cattle pioneers that contributed to agricultural development.

Okeechobee cattle auction

Fifty years ago in Florida, an acre of land sold for as little as $1.50. Ranchers began to buy the land and homestead; they gradually sold small corners off to dairy farmers to further develop and improve the fertility of the land. Then as the land was cured and fertilized, it was drained for the growth of farms and eventually sugar cane. Today, Pete Clemons, pioneer cattleman said it took the cattle to tame the land by pounding down the muck before vegetables and cane could be planted in the uncured slush. This natural progression from cattle to sugar cane still occurs today.

When Pete Clemons operated the livestock market in Belle Glade, there were eight slaughterhouses in Florida, now there is one. Today, most of the South Central Florida area cattle industry is involved in a feeder calf operation. There is one slaughterhouse in Florida with two packinghouses in nearby North and South Carolina and two in Georgia; three meatpacking companies Cargill, Con-Agra, IBP control 81% of the cattle raising market in the U.S.

The cattle business is small and underrepresented in Tallahassee and Washington, D.C. Pete Clemons said that most cattle people run mom and pop businesses demanding 24 hours, 7 days a week with little time left to lobby for the interests of the industry. Although Pete Clemons said, "Cattlemen need to do a better job promoting the industry to survive the ups and downs of a vulnerable and unpredictable business."

Clemons' dad worked for Irlo Bronson (who sold some land in Kissimmee to Disney) and helped develop the land at Venus where Pete Clemons was raised. He was brought up on the Bronson ranch and rodeoed fifteen years around the country. Irlo Bronson later became a State Senator making a fortuitous prediction early in his political career regarding the impact of economic development on the topography and hydrology of the land. He said that before they would finish channeling the Kissimmee River, people would say that it was a bad decision and it would end up being a political football. Another powerful legislative voice and a heritage of 150 years of ranching in Glades/Highlands County, Joe Peeples, Jr. reiterated the same belief in the 50's. Joe Peeples, Jr. at that time served in the Florida legislature and on the Southwest Florida Flood Control Board.

These statements continued to echo further south as the first cross country road, the Tamiami Trail (meeting at a "mistake" on 40 mile bend) from Miami to Naples began a contagion of interstate commerce. Later, Alligator Alley was "carved" across the heel of the Everglades linking drainage points further north, east and west across the peninsula that disrupted the natural flow of water from Lake Okeechobee.

Clemons predicts that the past is indicative of the future, as urbanization encroaches on agriculture interests with no turning back. A jaunt up Highway 27 to Clermont, now an extension of Orlando, reveals a "Stepford Wives" community taunting a million dollar country club, narrow lot lines where houses are separated by a "sneeze" on a warm night. New domed pool houses circle along groomed and heavily fertilized fairways with huge ponds spreading into the horizon transplanting rows of citrus trees and their fragrant orange blossoms that used to roll over the hills, lost to a freeze, grabbed up by urban developers.

In the 21st Century, environmentalists and Congress predict that restoring the vast Everglades "River of Grass" to its near pristine condition when Florida became a state in 1845 is possible. Already the move for Everglades Restoration is underway with the passage of an $8 billion dollar, 30-year Comprehensive Everglades Restoration Project (CERP). CERP construction projects are underway to restore the natural flow of water into Florida Bay and the South Florida aquifer. CERP is designed to restore the health of Florida's natural ecosystems while maintaining the levels of flood protection and water supply required by society. CERP was designed to achieve hydrologic performance goals considered to reflect 'healthy' ecological conditions. (The definition of a natural system is stated as all land and water managed by the federal government or the state within the South Florida ecosystem including: Water conservation areas; sovereign submerged land, Everglades National Park; Biscayne National Park; Big Cypress National Preserve, and other federal or state land designated and managed for conservation purposes; any tribal land designated and managed for conservation purposes as approved by the Tribe).

However, Pete Clemons doesn't believe that the Everglades can ever be restored; it is an ideological fantasy. How can Florida be restored after having been carved up north, south, east and west over the past Century? If the Everglades are restored to its natural state as in 1845 will the agricultural land and urban areas be returned to marsh and swamp?

After two decades of political maneuvering, CERP earmarked $243 million in fiscal year 2003 for acquisition of 170,000 acres in the agricultural community around Lake Okeechobee (the primary source of water for agribusiness), a loss of an estimated 60,000 acres of productive agricultural land to water storage. CERP is budgeted to compensate the counties circling Lake Okeechobee for properties taken off the tax rolls due to CERP, state/federal water conservation projects. Neighboring Henry County is expected to lose as much as $2 million in taxes. It is expected that land will be acquired by "eminent domain" should landowners refuse to sell river frontage property, the lifeblood of sustaining agriculture or cattle. However, even with great expectations, aquifer storage and recovery is controversial because it has only been in limited use. It is not known how the technology will impact water quality stored and recovered from the aquifers.

In Florida, the conflicting needs for water supply are complex with vast urbanization dominating the most influential economic need for water, as well as access to inland waterways for sports fishing, critical to sustaining the growth of the number one ranking industry: tourism. The blue gold "water" is in demand to supply the massive urban population explosion in South Florida expected to grow to by 12 to 15 million residents in the next 50 years. After two hundred years, the agri/cattle business is taking a backseat as a leading Florida industry.

Urban growth in Florida with a thousand people a day migrating into the state is a primary concern in the future. "With the new census defining Florida as the fourth most populous state in the nation (15, 982,378), issues regarding the use of "sustainable natural resources," i.e. the ability for the ecosystem to recharge itself and maintain stability, is not a new question. In Florida, law designates the South Florida Water Management District with a Mission "to manage and protect water resources of the region by balancing and improving water quality, flood control, natural systems and water supply. Its Vision: To be the world premier water resource agency." The South Florida Water Management District is the regulatory body that determines how land and water resources will be prioritized and apportioned.

The two most important natural resources in Florida are water and land. The three major economic sources in Florida competing for the non-renewable resources of land and water are: 1) Tourism 2) Construction/urban development 3) Agribusiness. Is there a solution to how these entities can co-exist?

Cattleman Pete Clemons is a reflective thinker with a wry sense of humor. He has his own way of looking at the influx of people into Florida and adds a biting quip: "Newcomers come to Florida bring with them $20, a change of clothes and never part with either of them." Since the end of the Pleistocene era over eleven thousand years ago with the first settlement by the Paleo-Indians, people have continued to follow the sun to Florida with a suitcase, suntan lotion, a change of clothes, a part-time job, and they stay.

The Glades County cow hunter whose heritage and lifeblood is ranching is becoming a myth, a disappearing breed in rural America. In Florida, the early settlers of the 1900's were agriculturalists and cow hunters, by 2003, 328 thousand jobs were lost from ranches and farms across the nation. Today, urbanization is bringing the extinction of a cultural heritage closer to reality.

THE DESTINY OF RURAL AMERICA

Woven throughout the patches of remaining small farms across the United States, the population is a global mix of nationalities, cultures, and urban and rural dwellers with vested interests in differing lifestyles. Perhaps a retort for contemplation on Florida's future for small farmers and ranchers is summed up applicably in a Pogo cartoon quoted by an anonymous agribusiness Sage: "We have met the enemy and he is us."

8

THE MUCK CITY EXPRESS

✦

PALMDALE

THE "HINKY DINKY" CHANGES THE FUTURE OF GLADES COUNTY

The crisp chilling air arches above the low-lying brush and curls the morning glories into the warmth of their fragrant cups. A blanket of dew-laden crystals spread across wide-open pastures, and even the cows huddle together for warmth. It is unusually cold with winds whistling the temperature down into chill bumps. It is a short invigorating walk to the little house nestled beneath tall oaks and branching arms that wear well their nearly century old age. These trees hold the secrets of the land but have always stood guard in this same spot as the new decade ushers in unredeemable changes to Palmdale in the heart of Glades County.

In the 1900's, it was the coming of the Iron Engine, the Atlantic East Coast Railway that brought the Future into the backyard of Glades County. With its smokestacks mounted high on its black-faced engine, huffing and puffing a dissipating curl of smoke into the wind, the engineer tugged out a special insignia whistle announcing its arrival. The train screeched to a slow grinding stop at the Palmdale depot to deposit another load of hopeful human baggage expecting to forge a life in this mysterious, unforgiving wilderness. Two of the men, who arrived later in the railroad's developing history in Palmdale to travel the rails through Glades County and far-reaching destinations, are former conductors Mike Haught and Joel Green.

Looking back into the Future that was yet to be written, Mike Haught and Joel Green recall stories that wrench laughter, tears and hair-raising fear about those unpredictable days when the black racer slithered through the town changing forever the lives of everyone along its iron path.

Before the coming of the railroad in the 1900's, roads were sunken grooves carved into muck, or they were an almost impassable swash cut through thick brush and sawgrass. Glades County emerged in the turn of the Century "boom days" as an outpost on the edge of the Everglades. Entrepreneurs arrived by road and river with big dreams of developing flourishing communities with glamorous hotels, cattle and agricultural farms to prosper from the "black gold" deposited around the edges of Lake Okeechobee. The "Muck City Express" and the "Hinky Dink" were unreliable means of transporting people to and from the DeSoto County center (before Glades County was splintered off in 1921 as the 58th county in Florida). However, transportation in and out of Palmdale was always difficult with most traveling by horseback or Model-T's on the high or low road of the "Tin Lizzie Trail" from Lakeport to Palmdale and Arcadia. Fisheating Creek was also an old artery to Lake Okeechobee and trading posts west to the Peace River.

In 1902, the "Garden of Eden" envisioned by Mr. Fogg with the Palmdale Land Company, (formerly the Florida Fruit Farm) was the first in a series of evaporating dreams. However, Palmdale did have its glamour days during the "boom times." In its heyday, Palmdale attracted worldwide tourists and buyers to explore the prospects of this "Garden of Eden." Ona Hendry remembers the classic high noon dining at the beautiful Palmdale Hotel located across the street from where the Palmdale Community Center is today (on Mainstreet).

But floods, drought and fires beat down the spirit of many aspirants and their hope to carve a living from the beautiful but hostile surroundings did not survive. With relentless "Will," some efforts of the pioneer homesteaders were rewarded for a time, only to be consumed repeatedly by the fury of Nature. Tough rawhide cattlemen, fortuitous fisherman, rugged individualists, and survivalist farmers somehow navigated through the perpetual wave of catastrophes, snakes, clouds of mosquitoes and stayed to build Glades County.

1900's—The bustling Palmdale depot

Eventually in 1917, after many of the homesteaders had given up hope and left, the Atlantic Coast Line Railroad was extended from Sebring into Palmdale. B. H. Whidden, related to pioneer cowboy Vance Whidden, was the first foreman. The Harrisburg railroad camp sprung up along the Creek named after the Harris Track Setter used to lay the first rails. The camp grew into a tent city of railroad workers and their families with births and deaths recorded during the time, as the Iron Engine's future began to take shape. The tent city later became the site of the now vacated Tom Gaskin's Cypress Knee Museum (in 1999, the State purchased the Gaskins' homestead property on the other side of Highway 27 and the family relocated the hand built Cypress structures to Tasmania. The only evidence where the homestead once perched above the clearing is the encroachment of the Everglades embracing its own).

When the railroad gained a foothold as a means of hauling freight and passengers through Glades County, the Atlantic Coast Line hub in Palmdale became a shipping point for cattle going to nearby slaughterhouses as well as a passenger line to points south. The train brought people from nearby towns for dances, political rallies and barbecues. Palmdale blossomed! There was a photo studio, a school, a general store, and post office. Palmdale even had oil prospectors that dug wells at Gopher Gully and Harness Pond, but the story goes that the well was dug too shallow to tap into the liquid gold. With today's technology, old timers believe that there still might be veins of oil silently waiting discovery deep in the Earth's hidden layers.

However, the railroad continued its track southward when in 1929, the first female Mayor of Moore Haven, Marion Horwitz O'Brien persuaded the owner of the rail, J. P. Morgan, to bring the train to her newly incorporated town. Somehow, the first passengers arrived at the Moore Haven depot some 19 miles south of Palmdale, bedraggled from unscheduled stops, the usual derailments and equipment failures. Catastrophes were normal problems that plagued passengers and freight in the Iron Horse days traveling across the ever-changing Everglades terrain. It was the coming of the railroad that was the initial finale of river transportation as a major means of trade and travel.

The railroad ownership changed hands frequently over the years. In 1961, when Mike Haught joined the line, it was called the Seaboard Airline until it merged with the Atlantic Coast Line and became the Seaboard Coast Line railroad. Joel Green signed on in 1957 when the rail was still the Seaboard Airline Railroad, later it became the Brandywine Valley, then the CXS Transport. Then in the 90's, U.S. Sugar bought the line.

During the heavy load seasons, the train hauled rock, local freight of pulpwood, dolomite and vegetables. The crew would "set off" the boxcars at sidings in Ortona, Goodno, Keri and Felda, Sears and Immokalee. They would leave the fully loaded boxcars to be emptied and then picked up on a return run. In what was termed the "perishable season," some of the vegetables that went on the Okeelanta line to Duda's in Belle Glade were stored in the world's largest walk in cooler until they could be hauled to their destination. During watermelon season, Mike Haught says that twice a week there was a piggyback service of two semis on flat beds trailing with more than a hundred cars to rush the vine ripe fruit to the New Jersey market on a deadhead three-day guaranteed delivery.

Joel Green and Mike Haught also served as brakemen, switching and pulling pens on the cars. Both say the work was hard and long, 16 hour days, 7 days a week, but "it was a lot of fun!" And, this is where the "stories" begin.

BELIEVE IT OR NOT!

When the two adventurers signed on at Palmdale, little did they realize that they had walked onto a stage in railroad history that required a test of endurance, physical strength, responsibility, brushes with fatal catastrophes, and the ability to remember a vast collection of epic stories to survive a lifetime. Their stories sound as if they were lifted from the pages of "Believe it or Not," but the two conductors attest to their validity. Haught and Green are as great at storytelling as they were railroad engineers, or what they called themselves: "the brains of the engine."

Former AEC train conductors—Joel Green and Mike Haught
"The brains of the engine!"

As the "yarns" unfold, Haught and Green use railroad lingo (practically another language to the uninitiated) to depict the crew and their jobs. Joel Green said the engineers were called "hog heads and the conductors rode the brain box of the train." Engineers were the railroad "firemen." With great laughter, the two conductors conspire an agreement "that the railroad firemen got their name from the steam engine days; they served on the steam engine until they cooked their brains out and that made then an engineer." The hierarchy of the crew positions is apparent in the humorous descriptions of Haught and Green, making light of the grueling team work necessary to get freight delivered on time to its destination and keep the freshest Florida vegetables and fruits on America's dinner tables.

Although truth is sometimes less believable than fiction, the tales of the railroad's history is rich with near calamities that are more humorous than tragic, as the tough little black steam engine huffed its way across Florida's heartland. Both Haught and Green stand pat on the details of one such story that allegedly occurred on the grade at Hall City. Apparently, a local farmer was pulling a tractor and a "chopper" over the crossing. The rig got stuck in the rails so the farmer attempted to pull a pin from the chopper in order to separate it from the tractor and clear the tracks. As he was struggling to get the two untangled, he heard an ominous whistle rapidly closing in on the crossing. The farmer is said to have launched a gigantic leap into the nearest bushes to clear the predicted impending disaster and the fate of the train.

Supposedly, a week later, someone asked the man what he was thinking when he heard the fast approaching train. Haught and Green said the man replied: "I thought this was going to be the darnist train wreck there ever was!" Although Haught and Green said that there were no serious injuries, they describe the engineer on the train as getting a drink of water at the time, not seeing the chopper on the tracks until he was upon it. When the two tons of metal engaged, the water cooler spewed water everywhere and landed the engineer upside down on his head as the train derailed. Haught and Green, enjoying more the embellishment of the story than the full disclosure of details, said the engineer "hid out in the woods for a week, then it took two more weeks and bloodhounds to find him before they could make out a report." (Reader discretion is required!)

Other stories Haught and Green detail are just as "believable." There were numerous uninvited guests that hitched a free ride on the train. The old term "hoboes" (originally used to describe people in the 20's who migrated across the United States in search of work) still jumped the train for a "ticket to ride." According to Haught and Green, "there was the time in the 60's when a group of youths climbed aboard in Immokalee wearing white flowing garb, piggybacking with a load of watermelons and oranges said to be their subsistent vegetarian diet." When they jumped off the train at Palmdale, Joel Green said he hollered down the line: "Casper ghosts were leaping off the back of the cars!" The rails officially delivered freight and unofficially delivered some seasonal workers with their dogs, families and belongings back home.

When the laughter dies down in-between stories, Haught and Green said, "The railroad was an adventure and a way of life that never dulled." During the "wild days," not specified here in terms of any exact time frame (names withheld to protect the innocent), Haught and Green said that there was one crewman who was fired for standing on a flat car hunting quail at the speed of a bullet as the train passed through the woods. The man would shoot the quail, then stop the train to retrieve his prize. The Game Warden is said to have discovered these antics, reported him, and the man received his official "traveling papers" from the railroad.

The run on the rails also attracted the circus, traveling minstrel shows, and movie stars that owned their own private boxcars. In the late 50's, when Jackie Gleason taped the "Honeymooners" at the Jackie Gleason Theatre in Miami Beach, he traveled the Seaboard train from New York City to the depot in Hialeah.

But, the dilemma of the rails was a continual saga confronting the conductors. In the early days, derailments were frequent due to the way the tracks were originally laid. At first, the tracks were laid on top of muck causing the tracks to be unstable and wiggle. This process involved digging a pit, for example in Palmdale, where they took out the dirt and put it on flat cars to build the Okeelanta branch near South Bay. They would lay the rail ahead of the train, push dirt to the sides, and then push the dirt underneath to pull up over the muck. There was about six inches of dirt laid over five feet of muck. Later, they dug canals on the sides and used lime rock to build up the rail beds to stabilize the tracks.

Since the railroad made its debut in the early 1900's, it became the lifeblood of America's commerce. Although the engines can still be heard echoing along Highway 27, the little defunct depots have either been preserved as an historical museum or disappeared all together. As Time speeds into the Future, there is never any turning back. Progress today is measured in technological leaps and bounds with the Past often an unrecognizable shadow in the Present. However, it doesn't mean that the past is ever forgotten as it is preserved in the epic tales and adventures passed down through time travelers who have lived and made the history of the rails come alive, like Mike Haught and Joel Green. Without the bravery and endurance of people who arch the Past to the Future, the gap of progress would not be bridged.

PALMDALE DEPOT LEFT TO THE TERMITES

During Palmdale's 1920's "boom days," The Atlantic East Coast Railroad's glistening white depot greeted weary travelers to the town. The picturesque little welcoming center, the gateway to Palmdale, was silenced when the town's commerce center faded. The little Palmdale train depot built by Jack Bass in the 1900's was in the 80's abandoned, deteriorated beyond preservation, eventually decomposed by termites and demolished.

The last steam engine that traveled the route from Palmdale to Sunnyland (12 miles south of Immokalee) to Copeland near Everglades City shut down in 1955. New faster engines evolved and were deployed to haul a variety of freight to points north and south with crews stationed in red "camp cars" at Palmdale for deployment elsewhere. One of the last "camp cars" used in the old days to house three rotating crews was retired alongside the Palmdale General Store and it too, eventually deteriorated.

Pausing along the railway spurs, now succumbing to rambling weeds taking back their domain, one can almost hear the ghostly huff of the AEC engine slowing its momentum into the station; instead, it is the grinding diesels of 18 wheelers echoing their hum of rubber down the highway. At the end of the day, what remains of the depot that once graced Palmdale is a rusted signal, bowing in silence beside the town's namesake, five spindly Palms reaching toward the sun, the only markers of the railroad's historic boom days.

Like it or not "change" is one of the few "always" of the world and life. Yet, a gnawing question persists: "What will the future bring to Glades County and how will lives and the wilderness be affected? The "forever" answer for Glades County is a question mark. As in the past, the fortitude and initiative of today's citizens will create and manifest the Vision of the Future.

THE PRISTINE WILDERNESS

Glades County is a unique gateway community; the central heartbeat of river, rail and roads weaving in all directions across the state. Glades County is one of the last pristine frontiers where the skies are dark, the cowboys ride the range, the woods sing with birds, trees are heavy laden with fruit and the black gold muck still gives the gift of life. In Glades County, the air is fresh, the wind can be heard whispering through the cabbage palms and oaks, there is still fish in the Creek, the Lake and the water is still the key lifeblood of the land. Decisions today on how these crossroads will intersect Tomorrow will write the destiny of Glades County.

Will the land and water remain in the guardianship of the citizens of Glades County or will the residents be evicted from the opportunity to preserve a non-renewable environment by those who want to carve up the land under the guise of "progress?"

Six spindly palms remain next to the train tracks where the Palmdale
Train Depot greeted travelers in the 1900's

9

THE LAST OF THE ROADSIDE ATTRACTIONS

✦

GATORAMA

One of the most familiar Florida landmarks, two miles south of Palmdale, is a national treasure. Gatorama, famous worldwide, representing a unique and disappearing culture in the United States of roadside tourist attractions. Before the days of turnpikes, U.S. 27 was the main diagonal road of travel across Florida; motorists had the opportunity to enjoy roadside attractions along the way from Miami, passing by Seminole Indian chickees, to "filling station" rest stops that displayed dens of hissing rattlesnakes for the amazement of tourists. Since laws have changed to protect the status of many Everglades wildlife, only a few species can be displayed under careful federal and state regulations. One of these exhibits is the Alligator.

Gatorama has experienced many up and down cycles in its history; however, it still stands at its original location founded by Cecil Clemons in the 1950's. Later the Gatorama namesake and business was purchased in 1986 by retired Army Officer Dave Thielen, who said with a bit a humor, "every Yankee wants to see an Alligator!"

Thielen, a "Florida Cracker" born in 1931 in Lakeport, felt that the alligator would be a curious attraction to northern visitors who had never before seen the gigantic reptile as they passed through Florida on heavily traveled U.S. 27. When the turnpikes and freeways carved new shortcuts across the state, some of the tourist trade was diverted, resulting in financial fluctuations. Today, Thielen's daughter and son-in-law, Allen and Patty Register, manage Gatorama.

Driving along Highway 27, a motorist's attention cannot help but be captured by the gapping mouth of a gigantic 40-foot alligator on a roadside billboard. When David Thielen returned to Florida after two tours of duty in Viet Nam, and was looking to establish a business in Glades County, he stopped at the familiar Gatorama he had passed a thousand times with the thought of purchasing the business. His wife, did not share so strongly his new idea, but later realized the revenue returns would justify the unique business venture. As the business grew, so did Thielen's family, with daughter Patty raised into the world of crocodiles and alligators ponds, monkeys, and panthers. While her friends were lugging a doll around on their hip, Patty toted her favorite pet monkey on her side.

In 1986, a Florida law was passed legalizing the farming of alligators (for meat and hides) that until then had been a lucrative, black market "poaching" business. With the passage of the law, breeding and raising alligators for meat and hides began the emergence of the alligator industry in Florida. In the 50's, when Cecil Clemons founded Gatorama, there were no regulations against taking alligators out of the wild for "exhibition stock" in captivity. However, in the 1960's, as the population of alligators began to decrease due to poaching and human encroachment on their environment, they became an endangered specie.

THE SCIENCE OF BREEDING ALLIGATORS AND CROCODILES

Today, the alligator population is explosive and alligator farming (breeding alligators in captivity) is regulated by the Florida Fish and Wildlife Commission. The evolution of the breeding side of the alligator industry began to emerge into a rapidly growing aquaculture business in South Florida, Georgia, and Louisiana. Allen Register is active in research and development of the Alligator Aquaculture Industry in Florida. He is chairman of the Florida Alligator Marketing and Education Advisory Council (FAME), appointed by the Commissioner of Agricul-ture to review budgetary allocations of funds for the aquaculture industry. Aquaculture is a new field that includes not only alligator farming but also the farming of tropical fish, catfish, crabs, shrimp and other specifies. Additionally, Allen is the coordinator for the alligator egg collection. As coordinator, Allen researches and analyzes data to determine how alligator farms can replenish their stock. The sale of alligator eggs is restricted to licensed growers and sell at $9.50 per egg. When purchasing an alligator egg, $5.00 is earmarked by the state for the development of the industry, and $1.00 of that amount goes to FAME. One of the annual functions of FAME is the collection of alligator eggs from the wild to replenish alligator breeder stock. Allen, whose expertise is also in the wetlands environment such as Gatorama where he breeds the alligators, says breeding in captivity is very difficult, thus, the stock from the wild assists in keeping the industry alive.

Allen Register unfurrows an incubating alligator nest.

Gatorama has become a foremost breeding center for a more than 4,800 alligators that began with an original clutch of only 400 Jamaican alligators. The alligators are harvested after two years when they reach about four and a half feet. The oldest alligator at Gatorama is 60 years old with the largest on site approximately fourteen feet long and 800 pounds.

Another aspect of the alligator industry of special interest to Patty Register is the development of "ecotourism" in Glades County. As a member of the Glades Economic Development Board, Patty recognizes the richness of the natural environment in which she was raised that today she appreciates even more as the wilderness in surrounding Everglades' counties is absorbed into urbanization. Historical preservation is also a strong interest of Patty, as both she and Allen are Florida Natives, raised into a fragile historical industry. But Gatorama represents a part of a disappearing American heritage: The roadside tourist attraction.

As a member of the Glades County Economic Development Committee, Patty has been exploring the "heritage tour" industry linking the historical sites across the country to the lucrative tourist trade. Towns, rich in pioneer history such as Palmdale, could become part of a traveler's destination guide to explore these last remaining examples of American history. Today, tourists seek vacation tours that lead them "back to nature," in a desire to return to the serenity of the natural environment as an escape from the overcrowded, noisy and hectic pace of the city. The new vacation packages promote cultural heritage tours as part of the wilderness exploration, to allow children to visit places where the pioneering spirit still exists in America.

In Palmdale, old town monuments like the Palmdale General Store, the Cypress Knee Museum and Gatorama are symbols that exhibit a lifestyle pioneers carved from the unforgiving forces of the Everglades to create a new life. The trend towards eco- and cultural preservation is like turning back a page back into history, moving forward and still preserving the founding fathers heritage within the natural environment and preserving the wilderness frontier as it is. (In 1999, the General store closed; the Cypress Knee Museum is deteriorating and the workshop was lost in a land battle).

Economic growth is high on the agenda for Glades County lawmakers. It is important to find a sustaining, clean industry that creates jobs, entices young people to stay, or return to the area, and contribute their talents to grassroots growth initiatives. Patty suggested collaborating with Florida Gulf Coast University to develop an eco-cultural heritage strategic business plan to assist the county in defining direction, goals and initiatives. One effort, the Lykes Brothers settlement agreement with the State was the preservation of 60,000 pristine wilderness acres along the corridors of Fisheating Creek as part of the Wildlife Management Area to prevent development. Patty Register emphasized that the time is "ripe" for considering preservation ideas as rapid development encroaches upon surrounding Everglades' counties.

But Patty and Allen's main focus is on their everyday business of meeting tourists, guiding them through Gatorama and answering a thousand questions about their resident alligators and crocodiles. At the gift shop, visitors can purchase leather goods, shell crafts, alligator novelettes and even custom made alligator shoes. Whether or not a person is a Native Floridian or a tourist from the far corners of the world, Gatorama offers a memorable experience that lures people back time and again to rediscover the ancient living descendents of the dinosaur. Gatorama is open Monday through Saturday 8–6 p.m. and Sunday, 10–6 p.m.

ALLIGATOR SCIENCE LAB

The science of alligator farming is a unique business. Patty and Allen Register have been living with alligators and crocodiles for over ten years. The Register children, Erica and Benjamin, have had the fascinating opportunity to eat breakfast overlooking their huge backyard pond watching the antics of the reptilians whose ancestry dates back more than 200 million years to the ancient dinosaurs. The nature of the alligator and crocodile, both native to Florida, is not only observed by the Register family but is also studied as a science and industry.

Gatorama's reptilian research is a "hands-on" science managed with meticulous care by Allen Register. When Allen met Patty in Haines City where they grew up, he went off to serve in the Navy submarine fleet, then returned to Florida. His interest in alligators and crocodiles was yet to be cultivated. However, when Thielen turned over the management of Gatorama to the Registers, Allen established his credentials in the field of alligator management through his work. Allen's expertise in wetland habitat where Gatorama is located, affords him and Patty the opportunity to live with and observe the reptiles in their natural setting. Allen and Patty research, breed and harvest alligators in what is becoming a lucrative new Florida industry: Aquaculture.

Allen is chairman of the Florida Alligator Marketing and Education Council appointed by the Commissioner of Agriculture, as well as a member of the

Aquaculture Advisory Board of the State of Florida that provides budgetary recommendations for the industry.

As the visitor walks on the boardwalk through Gatorama, crocodiles, alligators and humans peer at each other from a safe distance. The reptiles float their posture with part of their spiked tail above the water line, giving a sense of the size of the creature, as the eye travels toward the triangular head of the crocodile or rounded muzzle of the alligator's snout. Patty explains that there are two species of alligators: Chinese (endangered) and American. Gatorama began with a clutch of 800 alligators that today has expanded to more than 4500. In 1968, Gatorama added the Jamaican Crocodile to the attraction before they were an endangered species. The crocodile is not farmed, but only exhibited at the farm. The crocks and gators are separated from each other and nest in different areas.

Alligators and crocodiles have similar, yet different nesting patterns. Crocodiles create a two-chambered nest and burrow in a 20–30 foot area. The female crocodile finds just the right spot then digs down about 24 inches before laying all of the eggs in a pocket, except one. The last egg is laid on top then covered with a thin layer of earth. This is the mother crocodile's sacrifice for the survival of her clutch. The one egg is a "lure" for predators to devour the contents and move on, saving the nest until the hatchling stage, another "survival of the fitess" challenge. There are nine species of crocodiles at Gatorama, and as Patty describes, most people do not realize that crocodiles are native to Florida. Gatorama exhibits crocodiles to educate the public on their ancestral history, breeding habits and behaviors to better understand a reptile they may never have seen before and know little about.

Alligators have a somewhat different nesting behavior than crocodiles. The female alligator builds a nest out of surrounding vegetation and brush that is piled in a high mound to protect the eggs she lays. Patty and Allen collect alligator eggs from the nest and incubate them in a special 100% humidified shed. The eggs incubate for a period of approximately 60 days for the alligator, and 90 days for the crocodile. Before the hatchling breaks through the egg, the embryo floats to the top as a white band encircles the egg. The new hatchlings are not much larger than the palm of the hand but already the razor sharp teeth are poised to snap down on any imposing object. Luckily, their aggressive bite as a hatchling feels about as sharp as that of a kitten.

The alligator grows about one foot a year to nearly six feet, while crocodiles can become much larger. The biggest crocodile at Gatorama is 15 feet long and weighs approximately 1500 pounds. The largest alligator weighs 800 pounds and is approximately 13–14 feet long. At Gatorama, alligators are harvested for meat and hide at two years, when the gator is about 4 1/2 feet long. Their hides are processed, tanned and made into belts, wallets, novelettes, purses and shoes that can be purchased at Gatorama. For alligator shoes, ladies, be prepared to bring some extra cash!

Although alligator meat is considered a delicacy in many parts of the country, in Palmdale it is available fresh every day with raw alligator tail meat selling for $8.50 a pound.

Patty and Allen Register view the Aquaculture Industry in Palmdale and Florida as a growing business with limitless economic potential. This is one opportunity already being developed at Gatorama. Additionally, the latest trend in "ecotourism" and "cultural heritage tours," offers Palmdale and Glades County a head start on the development and growth of this environmentally friendly industry. Palmdale's heritage is its pioneer history, offering an opportunity for a "revival" tourist business.

The Wildlife Management Area at the Palmdale Campground preserves the natural beauty along Fisheating Creek for primitive camping, hiking, nature tours, canoeing, and seasonal hunting. The opportunity for Palmdale and Glades County residents to capture the lucrative tourist trade can provide new jobs in an industry that protects the wilderness and safeguards the beauty of the Everglades environment. But it is a daunting challenge to the new pioneers in the age of Florida's explosive population growth.

Palmdale has not changed drastically from the days of the Palmdale Land Company when it was known as the "Tin Lizzie Trail to the Garden of Eden." Today, Palmdale still deserves that reputation, if local interests develop businesses that can revive the economy, capitalizing on its historic heritage and environmental roots. Patty Register, who serves on the Economic Development Board of Glades County, believes "the opportunity is now."

In the meantime, Palmdale is closed. It is a ghost town.

10

"MADE DO, WOULD DO, COULD DO"

◆

THE GLADES COUNTY LEGACIES

"THE BIG ONE THAT DIDN'T GET AWAY" WORLD FAMOUS FISHING GUIDE: RAY DONALD THIELEN—MOORE HAVEN

Ray Donald Thielen, niece Patty Register and his wife, Margie, relax in
Moore Haven surrounded by his fishing trophies

"This is the end of the Earth," exclaimed Ray Donald's Missouri born mother when she traveled in a Model-T with her husband to take a job at the Killgorn Seed Company in Florida. It wasn't exactly the AAA route of roadside motels, as the early pioneers had to camp alongside the soggy muck laden roads, fighting off black clouds of mosquitoes, and sleeping in humidity soaked clothes clinging to the body like a second skin. The early 1900's were harsh days for the early Glades pioneers not knowing what to expect as they trudged through the tall palmettos, cypress strands, and snake-invested swamps. But the early "Florida Crackers" were people with grit, determination and stamina, or else they did not survive the trials and tribulations of Florida's harsh welcome mat. Ray Donald's family came to Florida and stayed with Ray Donald becoming one of the great Lake Okeechobee freshwater fishing guides.

Ray Donald was a 1926 hurricane baby born in Sebring and raised in Lakeport. Ray Donald remembers the stories of his parents after the disaster when the family of ten began to rebuild their lives raising cattle, horses and corn. Ray Donald's childhood was filled with adventure and struggle. The Thielen children moved into a "pre-fabricated" house; Mother Thielen used her creative talent to stitch together clothes for the kids from sugar, flour and cattle feed sacks to go to school. However, each morning before the kids were bussed from Lakeport to Moore Haven's one room school house, the children helped their dad milk the cows, strain the milk through corn sacks filled with ice to keep it cold. Mrs. Thielen would begin the daily churning of milk into butter and cottage cheese, while the children fed the cats "a la natural" from the warm utters of the cows. Some milk was also saved for the calves as it contained strong antibodies for prevention of the prevalent host of animal diseases that lurked in the Everglades.

Before school, the kids would collect frogs caught the night before, iced down in burlap bags and mosses to prepare them for delivery to the fish house where they were sold. One of Ray Donald's little brothers, David, attached to the nickname "Frog" (perhaps he was the best of the frog trouncers), returned to Palmdale after serving in the Army and opened the famous roadside landmark Gatorama on U.S. 27 in Palmdale.

As a teenager, Ray Donald's sparkle for life captured the eye of another teen, Margie Nell, whose courtship ended in a lifelong marriage since she was 16 years old. Margie Nell says she was a "Georgia Cracker" but now considers herself a "Florida Native." Ray Donald's bride joined him in his cattle drives and supported him in his fishing guide business.

Ray Donald says that he and Palmdale pioneer Tom Gaskins, Senior used to compete every year in the turkey-calling contest at the annual Chalo Nikka (King of Bass) Festival. Ray Donald carved the famous turkey callers and looked forward to the yearly battle to win the title of "Master of the Glades County Turkey Callers." Ray Donald became associated with the Glades County Hunting Club and soon began to ply his fishing guide skills with sportsman interested in catching the big bass on the Big Lake. Ray Donald talks of the early days of Hall City and Citrus Center, where big game hunters from the northeast would meet at the picturesque Citrus Center Hotel; a two story wooden frame structure with the traditional roundabout Florida screened porch, peering out over the Everglades wilderness. The graceful hotel seemed so foreign to the rugged environment, as if it was plucked from some sandy beach on the eastern seashore and transplanted into the rich black-gold Everglades muck. Not only did Citrus Center attract game hunters, it also attracted the "hunted." There are epic stories about the convict camp nearby where it is said a "still" was in full swing making alcohol during the 13 months of prohibition.

The Depression hit Florida hard and reached its tentacles into the limited economy of Glades County throughout the early 40's. Ray Donald joined the Navy in World War II as a spotter for German or Japanese aircraft off the Florida coast. Later, when the Korean War broke out, Ray Donald served on the crash crew team for fighter pilots at the training center in Jacksonville where cadets learned how to land and take off from aircraft carriers. Ray Donald remembers some of the tragic events of pilots who didn't make it through the training and lost their lives. Ray Donald, clad in an asbestos suit, had to dive into mangled, blazing cockpits in a desperate attempt to rescue the injured young men. After Korea and the reduction in military forces, Ray Donald took a job in Stuart, Kissimmee, and Moore Haven as a "Lock" man.

However, Ray Donald always followed his love for fishing and his reputation as a fishing guide began to spread; he became known as one of the best Lake Okeechobee fishing guides in Florida. His career attracted clients such as Sammy Snead and baseball's Ted Williams. Ray Donald's ability to "smell out" the fishing holes in Lake Okeechobee was often described as "uncanny." No one yet has ever learned his secret, and he doesn't reveal much about this acute "second sense," but all of the great sport fishermen knew he could trick the cagiest of bass and lure them right onto the angler's bait and into the frying pan. People have traveled from all over the world to hire the guide services of Ray Donald. In 1960, he acted as the angler's guide for the first world series of fishing in the Freshwater

Division and proudly displays the plague dated January 19, 1960, one of many awards mounted on the backdrop of his dining room china cabinet. If you were to review Ray Donald's client list, it would resemble a Hollywood "Who's Who" of all the celebrities for whom he has brought home the "big one" from the clear, silent waters of Lake Okeechobee.

Ray and Margie live along a quiet street in Moore Haven, in warm, comfortable rooms garnished with souvenirs from around the world, symbolic of their unique lifestyle. Ray Donald has traveled the world but loves best his own backyard: Lake Okeechobee. He has fished with the best of sportsman, and tells some very tall, but real, "fish tales." However, instead of the usual stories of fishermen who talk about "the big one that got away," his globetrotting clientele can attest to the fact that for Ray Donald, "the big one never got away!"

Legendary fishing guide, Ray Donald Thielen passed away, January 2003.

THE HENDRY FAMILY
PALMDALE

The legacy of the Hendry family is interwoven into the fabric of Florida's Wilderness history. The family for which a county is named provides a colorful glance back into the early days of Palmdale's "boom and bust" heritage.

Sitting in Pete Hendry's family room is like visiting a Florida pioneer museum. The overstuffed shelves are filled with memorabilia, old books, novelties collected from around the world with two criss-crossed World War II Japanese swords mounted above the brick fireplace mantel. All of these mementos record the life and times of Peter and Ona Hendry, who came to Palmdale 45 years ago.

The Hendry ancestry, on Pete Hendry's side, traces back to the 1770's with the migration of settlers searching for a better life in America. The first three Hendry brothers crossed-the ocean from Scotland then made their way south to homestead in Georgia. In order to make a living, Robert Hendry, along with sons William and John, began to farm cotton and corn on their large southern plantation; Robert Hendry is the great, great, great, great grandfather of Pete Hendry and his son, John Hendry, the great, great, great grandfather of Pete Hendry. John Hendry was one of the first born in America in 1778. Eventually, the John Hendry family migrated to Hamilton County, Florida where he lived and died. During this Civil War the Hendry family began to trickle down through the woods of Northern Florida as they ventured southward to the harsher marshlands and prairie of Central Florida. At this time, the total population of Florida was about 70,000.

Pete Hendry's family relocated near Palmdale from North Florida in 1859. They settled around Wauchula and Arcadia working the sawmill. Pete Hendry was born in Moore Haven in 1924, growing up in the aftermath of floods and hurricanes. As a young man of 15, he began to ramble. He plied a trade as a cow hunter and secured other jobs during his roaming days. Forty-five years ago, Hendry came to Palmdale to visit a WWII buddy from a German war camp; Ona's brother. Pete Hendry said, "It was love at first site!" Ona Hendry captivated Pete Hendry and the two were married. Hendry began to buy up property from some of the widely scattered Palmdale Land Company holders and acquired a large amount of Glades County acreage. Ona and Pete endured the many cycles of natural disasters of the ever-changing Everglades, and remained to live and raise a family. The Hendry family kin still hold one of the largest family reunions in Florida.

Ona Hendry, from Kenansville, Florida, another historic town north of Yeehaw Junction, attracted the keen eye of Pete Hendry when he returned from World War II. Although Pete Hendry does not like to speak about it, he was a decorated hero, serving in the Combat Engineer Corp in the Ruhr Valley, Germany and in Japan. Ray Hendry, his son, is also a decorated Viet Nam hero and lives in Palmdale with his family at the Sabal Palm campground they own.

The early Hendry pioneers branched out into several areas of Florida and becoming one of the few families so recognized by the naming of a legislative area: Hendry County. Spessard Stone, who has researched the lengthy genealogy of the Hendry's and authored books on Florida history, writes that one of the Hendry family clan, Trace Stone, was one of the first President's of the Florida Legislative Council in 1826; Florida became a state in 1845. Trace Stone was the great grandfather of Henry Stone whose wife was a Hendry and the daughter of Baptist minister Reverend James "Boss" Hendry. It was Stone who named the town "Arcadia," where he settled with his large family of 17. The Baptist ministry traditionally runs in the Hendry family, including Pete Hendry who was a Sunday school teacher for more than 30 years, and founded the Palmdale Baptist church. Ona and Pete held church services in their home until they finished the major accomplishment of building by hand the church. The church steeple still stands tall above the skyline of trees and houses, the only church in the heart of Palmdale.

PALMDALE BUILDS A CHURCH

The first and only church in Palmdale—1999

Since the early days of Florida's history, the first structure to rise above the tree-tops was the church steeple, a visible symbol that a new community was coming to life. In Palmdale, it was not until 1966 that the town had its very own church: The Palmdale Baptist Church. The pioneering spirit that inspired the early homesteaders to survive the ever-changing moods of Nature's fury on the edge of the Everglades drew the people of Palmdale together to build its first church.

As Pete Hendry tells the story, every man in Palmdale gave money to build the Palmdale Baptist Church on Seminole and 5th Street, in the heart of the town. A man in Ft. Myers provided the original small white frame building, topped with a steeple and brass bell that calls people to service on Sunday. The original white wooden building stands in front of newer streamlined buildings added since the church was established and the population expanded. Former pastors of the Venus Baptist church donated funds to construct the original Palmdale church with additional money sent from pastors in nearby states.

But, church services began in Palmdale several months before the people had their own building. Pete Hendry, born in Venus, was a Sunday school teacher for

31 years. When he and his wife Ona moved to Palmdale, Pete had hopes of building a church to "lead people to the Lord and a Christian life." In October of 1965, Ona and Pete Hendry fulfilled their dream to provide Palmdale with church services when they opened their own home for Sunday worship. For six months, they held church services until the townspeople envisioned the dream of a permanent home for the Baptist church and the people of Palmdale. Mr. and Mrs. Lanier (parents of the former County Commissioner Debbie Mann who succumbed to cancer August 22, 1998), Brother Riddle, a pastor from Moore Haven, Doug Swan and his brother, William Milton "Bud" Hendry, and jack-of-all-trades Ona Hendry built the church from the ground up. Six months later, in 1966, Palmdale had its own spiritual center. The Palmdale Baptist Church has an average of 45 members under the ministry of Reverend William R. Flury who has served there for 14 years. His wife Francis and two daughters came to Palmdale from Everglades City where Reverend Flury was a pastor for nine years.

One of the church's big events is the traditional annual "homecoming," when everyone is invited to attend the special services and a community lunch. Reverend Flury says on the last Sunday of the month, the Palmdale Baptist Church holds special services beginning at 10 a.m. with a potluck lunch and fellowship in the afternoon. One of Palmdale's own son's, Reverend Jimmy Snell returned one Sunday to present the "homecoming message." Hugh Snell, Jimmy Snell's Uncle, told Pete Hendry "the church built in Palmdale was the best thing that ever happened." The monthly homecoming event provides an opportunity to revive community spirit.

In today's world, a concern for youths is a focal point of all religious denominations. Reverend Flury says there are a lot of young people in Palmdale, but the attraction of outside entertainment draws a greater interest for youths than attending church. He says the church has tried many programs over the years to involve young people in church activities, as have other churches across the country, but new programs with a high successful appeal are in demand.

Reverend Flury always holds out the welcome mat to anyone to come to the weekly services. Every Sunday, the steeple bell chimes through the town calling everyone to the little sparkling white Palmdale Baptist Church, the only church in town.

THE REST OF THE HENDRY CLAN

The Hendry family history is long and spreads out across Florida. Becky Hendry founded "Sav the Creek" Foundation and headed up the ten-year legal battle against Lykes Brothers to establish Fisheating Creek as a public, navigable waterway. The result was the State establishing 60,000 acres as a Wildlife Management Area along the corridors of the Creek for primitive camping, canoeing, hunting and air boating in designated areas. Becky Hendry's father is Pete Hendry's great uncle related by marriage.

"Sav the Creek"—Fisheating Creek closed to the public

Ella Kathryn Hendry just published a book on Hendry genealogy. She wrote the book as a tribute to her brother Harry Hendry, who died in 1945 in the Battle of the Bulge. The book is entitled FRONT PORCH STORIES: TALES OF THE HENDRY FAMILY PIONEERS IN FLORIDA'S PEACE RIVER BASIN. Jonathan Nilson Sandige, P. O. BOX 2594, PORT CHARLOTTE, FL 33949, publishes the book.

Pete and Ona Hendry's old style Florida home is nestled beneath the natural beauty of tall oaks just as they were when the Hendry's first fell in love with the land. The Ray Hendry family also lives at the Campground and often hosts special benefits with blue grass music, dancing and homemade barbecue cooking by Palmdale residents. Ray Hendry also supplies rental canoes at the Palmdale General Store and Café for peaceful trips down Fisheating Creek. Ray and his wife are also involved with the Ultra Light Association that just opened a charter chapter in Palmdale. The Ultra Lights can be rented for a beautiful flight above the meandering Creek and wilderness area. The Ultra Lights are housed at the Sabal Palm Campground hangar. Flights can be arranged at the campground.

THE GARDEN OF EDEN

Fisheating Creek

One of the first developers in Glades County was the Florida Fruit and Farms Company out of St. Louis, Missouri, of which the Palmdale Land Company was a subsidiary. In 1918, according to Pete Hendry, the company developed 37 subdivisions in Glades County. There were three town sites, Palmdale, Alfred City and Allentown, one-mile square townships; the only remaining one today is Palmdale. Through a nationwide marketing campaign, especially targeted at people in the Mid-Atlantic States, the curious invested cash in the promotional land deal that pitched the idea that in Palmdale "you can grow corn ten feet high!" The land was promoted as not only possessing the "black gold" soil but also oil. A period of real or imagined flurry of oil drilling expeditions returned no results based on the 1900's technology. The oil wells were capped and deserted.

As the Palmdale Land Company pursued its development of "The Garden of Eden," they divided acreage into lots, and called in the government surveyors. Pete Hendry describes the unique method of determining lot sizes. A knot was tied onto a wagon wheel and footage determined by how many times the wheel rolled over. Pete Hendry describes this as this method by which government surveyor, Isaac Thornton in 1859, set-aside streets and dedicated public rights of ways in the townships. The plat books in Moore Haven reveal the roadways that carve through Palmdale's palmetto covered properties, owned by people from all over the United States. Pete Hendry and his wife Ona, are linked to these early days when 30 years later, after the depression in 1935, 18 cents bought an acre of land in Glades County.

In the early 1900's when the Palmdale Land Company plotted out the boundaries for the townships, the construction of the Palmdale Hotel began in order to house visitors who came to look over the "for sale" property.

Ona Hendry remembers her days as an employee at the hotel when she helped with the chores and hosted arriving visitors dropped off at Florida East Coast Railway depot to take a look at the wilderness land. Roads were then rugged, with travelers from Moore Haven bumping along the old grade behind the Gaskins' property on horses and buckboards. There were also the Indian Drive Trucks with chain wheels that could trudge across the muck land, most of the time without sinking, and provided a practical form of transportation. Nevertheless, in 1918, people traveled from all parts of the early sprouting townships in Florida to visit Mrs. Ahler's Palmdale Hotel. The railroad crews at Harrisburg, next to Fisheating Creek, were also guests at the two-story building that towered above the flatlands.

The times in Palmdale brought continuous change, yet new arrivals came by train and wagon on a continual stream, each homesteader buying land and later deserting it in crucial weather or financial conditions. Either the ground was too dry, or too wet, or transportation was too difficult in and out of Palmdale. One of Palmdale's early survivors, Pete Cruise bought one of the still standing, oldest houses in Palmdale.

Cruise bought the house from the original owner, Dr. Snell in the 1890's. The pine house remains almost as it was originally built with the traditional screened porch for cross-ventilation of summer breeze throughout the rooms off the corridors. Harley Thomas, who tells the history of his house, now lives under the shade of the huge Fichus, as did his former occupants, tucked away down a dirt road off Main Street. In the 1800's, however, the landscape was far less dry. Thlothlopopka-Hatchee, the Indian word for "stream where fish eat," twisted along the township with clumps of cabbage palms, cypress heads, cattails, ferns and water lilies, made manageable for travelers with heavy wheeled carts, "the Muck City Express" or flat-boats poling through the extended swamp prairie of the Everglades. The hammocks provided the only dry ground as a respite from the ever-sinking Everglades muck.

SURVIVING THE EVERGLADES REVENGE

In 1926, Florida's most destructive natural disaster devastated many of the burgeoning townships arising around Lake Okeechobee. Moore Haven, at the south end of the Lake, was virtually wiped out. The land rush development in Citrus Center (off U.S. 27 to Ortona) and its tourist hotel, an attraction to wealthy northerners, disappeared. After the 1926 hurricane, many disillusioned people moved on rather than survive the hardships of living in makeshift tents, fighting hordes of mosquitoes and snakes all seeking food and higher ground. Some people reported snakes coiling along the now low-lying ceilings, with dead fish and cattle polluting the surrounding water with rotting carcasses. Only the formidable remained to reclaim the territory and the rich aftermath of enriched hurricane saturated soil.

Throughout the years of land promotions to develop Glades County, Nature played havoc. Colonies of settlers disappeared as quickly as they arrived, one wave after the other. Each small land development in and around Fisheating Creek experienced a brief revival of prospectors hoping to derive a new life and live off the promise of the land and Lake Okeechobee. Fisherman, cattlemen and truck farmers, rotated their prosperity dependent on the natural fluctuations of the environment.

In 1951, a flood struck Palmdale. A lengthy deluge or torrential rains flooded the entire town as the headwater of Fisheating Creek in Venus flowed down State Road 25 through the famous Oasis Bar and Restaurant. The small wooden structure was waterlogged during the continual downpours with the Creek overrunning the wooden floors, doors and through the windows of the little red shadow box diner. This, too, soon passed and the doors once again opened for business.

Palmdale's early pioneers traveled through the town, stayed or settled nearby. The legacy of the pioneering families of the Hendrys', the Whiddens', the Peeples', the Gaskins', and unnamed others, as well as the early Seminoles of the Brighton Reservation who followed in the footsteps of Chief Billie Bowlegs, are the motley composite of a history that is old, yet forever being renewed. The families that remain are still cultivating the land, and surviving the ever-changing environment to carve a future. The value of the pioneering heritage is a handed-down knowledge and understanding of this unique land. The fragile human lives, shaped by the fickle changes of flood and drought have toughened over the years. Some of the original homesteaders, who stepped off the Florida East Coast Railway in satin, high-heeled shoes and high silk hats, were educated by the hardships of surviving the Everglades frontier. The plume feathers, taken from delicate egrets that foraged the soil in huge colorful bands and adorned the hats of the ladies at the Palmdale Hotel, were soon traded for wide brimmed riding hats, leather boots, horses to ply through muck and thickets of heavy palmettos. Through fires, human and cattle epidemics, as well as other unpredictable scourges across the land, the pioneering families "made do, would do and could do," an old Florida Cracker epitaph.

The 1951 flood covers the highway into Palmdale

Today, the only remains of the Palmdale Hotel are incorporated into the walls of the deceased Bill Arnold's house (whose sister is Ona Hendry) and occupied by Arnold's daughter, Gloria. Arnold bought the hotel after it closed down and built his house on the site out of the wooden frame. The giant oak tree that shades most of the landscape marks the historic grounds of the used to be thriving hotel in Palmdale's heyday.

The old oak tree shades the Arnold home built upon the site of the Palmdale Hotel

Ona Hendry's fond memories of the hotel, recalls the days when homemade garden vegetables and cookies were served at noontime to visitors who enjoyed the atmosphere of the wilderness. The Palmdale Hotel reveals the elegance attributed to those who envisioned the promise of "The Garden of Eden."

THE END OF THE DAY

The sky now turns a purple haze, the pattern since time memorial, as the heat of the day collects in the summer clouds. The birds flutter into the protection of the oaks, predicting on the wind, the smell of Nature's onslaught. The air chills, and the breeze pauses. A distant rumbling gradually echoes louder across the prairie as the sky darkens the sun. Only in the Everglades can the drama of an approaching storm bring one so close to Nature's mysterious and unrelenting force. Suddenly, as if by surprise, the sky froths with torrential downpours, lightning electrifies the air bolting to ground zero through the heart of a tree as it travels, in a split second, to some untold reservoir deep within the Earth's dark core. Alas, the drought stricken ground drinks in the long awaited rain bursting forth from the full-bellied clouds. The rain pounds on the tin roofs of stables, trailers and homes alike; there is nothing left to do but listen and wait. Just as quickly as Nature unleashes the relentless cleansing rain, the sun returns. The trees let go of the birds, the sweet smell of freshness rises up through the brush, the Everglades releases its creatures back to the land and the natural cycle continues. Man only visits here with Nature in a perpetual legacy to survive and preserve, as did the Ancestors in awe of the Everglades' wonders.

For those who poled here by canoe, trudged the prairie in wagons, Tin Lizzies or the AE Railway, the Glades County history of Palmdale is forging onward. Who knows the legends of Palmdale's future? What will the "new" pioneers carry forth from the legacy of the 1900's? What will be remembered, what will be forgotten? What legends of the past will be forged as Palmdale's legacy in the 21st Century? Who will carry the torch of Florida's legendary wilderness heroes into the "living" future? Perhaps the Ancestors will speak to the Wind, as the Indian lore describes, to rekindle the spirit of the living in the virtual ghost town of Palmdale. The future is yet to be written by those who remain.

THELMA COOK: THE FIRST WORKING WOMAN
MOORE HAVEN

Someone once made the comment to Thelma Cook that it was "bad" for women to work, but those words never deterred her from pursuing a 30-year career that began in Moore Haven at the B & B grocery story. Thelma was promoted to Manager and remained Assistant Manager for 30 years before her retirement. During the 1940's, coming out of the Depression, a job meant providing the family with a supplemental income to her husband's work as a Lock Tender at

Ortona. On August 26, 1999, Thelma celebrated her 84th birthday, a life that spans from 1916 through two World Wars, the Depression into the Technological Age that exploded on the scene with the invention of the wireless, first radio and telephone in the 20's. Moore Haven got its first telephone system in 1920.

Thelma Cook and son Tommy at home in Moore Haven

Thelma married her husband Titus in 1929 who came to Moore Haven from Clewiston and later took a job working in the "broom straw business." C. O. Hickok's Broom Factory supplied the brooms (made from broomcorn raised in the area), to local packinghouses, the cannery and other Moore Haven businesses. The Cooks' have two sons, Tommy and Edward. Tommy recalls their early life in the 40's when Moore Haven was just a one room schoolhouse, hotel, bank, post office, bar and restaurant. The Cooks' arrived in Moore Haven after the big boom days when the town had several grand hotels, a pharmacy, and a booming fish industry.

As a child, Thelma Cook grew up surrounded by the sweet aroma of citrus blossoms in Hicoria, Florida. Her father was one of the first citrus growers, and she loved the freedom of running between the rows of trees on the homestead property of her Grandmother and Uncle. Thelma lived in Sebring and Avon Park then moved to Moore Haven where she met her husband who lived just down the street.

THE GOOD OLD DAYS IN MOORE HAVEN

Moore Haven began as a vision of Seattle hotel magnate, James A. Moore who bought 98,000 acres of flat top cypress land to be developed by the Florida Land Company. It was the navigability of the Caloosahatchee from the west coast to Okeechobee that was the impetus to the town's growth. Moore Haven was difficult to reach by land as the old Model-T's and buggies had to navigate through the palmetto patches, soggy muck with the constant threat of becoming stuck somewhere in transit in the middle of nowhere. However, Moore Haven was destined to grow as early land developers foresaw a great economic resource in the virgin Everglades. Several developers competed to lure adventurous spirits to buy into their vision with cold hard cash. Other land companies such as the Palmdale and the Chicago Land Company that developed Citrus Center were advertising across the United States and Europe to attract residents to the newly "paper drafted" Florida communities. Matter of fact, when people arrived at their dream plot of land, they wound up living in tents until living quarters were constructed. By the time Thelma Cook moved to Moore Haven, the town was at the end of its glory days; the 1926 Hurricane and onset of the Depression was a staggering blow to the town in death toll and economics. The doldrums lasted more than a decade. However, Tommy Cook has happy childhood memories of Moore Haven and especially remembers Ms. Stalls the teacher at the one room schoolhouse in Ortona. One of the graduating classes from Moore Haven High School had only five boys and eight girls. Tommy says, "Originally the school was located behind the jail and the jail was the old football field. The town had no streetlights and the roads were dirt but there was plenty of room in this quiet little town where you could know everybody since the town was mostly isolated." Tommy liked Moore Haven and still lives there today.

Because Tommy's dad worked as a lock tender for the Water Management District, the family followed his work to Canal Point, Citrus Center, Okeechobee and Orotona. Titus and another Glades County pioneer, Ray Donald Thielen both worked at the Ortona lock that was constructed in 1936. In 1942, Thelma and the family moved into a one-room apartment above Main Street's bar that Tommy remembers being much larger than the small living quarters at Canal Point even though there was only one light bulb, a kerosene water heater and a shared bathroom down the hall. In the 40's, meat was scarce as well as sugar, gas and leather that were rationed to residents. Tommy recalls that they ate canned calf meat due to the shortage and as Thelma comments, "people had to watch every penny to survive."

Tommy and his brother enjoyed a childhood in the wide-open spaces surrounded by the tall sugar cane and lots of opportunity to fish. Thelma used to buy five fifty gallon drums of oil to cook for the first Chalo Nitka festival still celebrated today with rodeos, crafts and Indian fry bread.

THE FIRST WOMAN MAYOR IN MOORE HAVEN

Thelma Cook was a vision of the 40's woman following a tradition set by the first Mayor of Moore Haven, a woman named Marian Newhall Horwitz O'Brien elected in 1917. Mayor O'Brien came to power almost by "default" when no one else wanted the job and a time in Florida when only men had the right to vote if they paid a poll tax. Her election as one of the first female Mayors in the United States gained nationwide publicity. Mrs. O'Brien also set another precedent for women as a sophisticated lady of fashion. Mayor O'Brien was often photographed in her feather plumed satin hat, ruffled blouse and long satin skirt cinched in the middle to emphasize the glamorous tiny waist of the time. Even though Moore Haven was just a blink in the eye on the far edge of urban life, on special occasions the women were fashionably elegant. Poised with her friend Pat Taylor, grandmother of Holly Whiddon the Supervisor of Elections, Thelma Cook and her friend were captured in a 1900's snapshot wearing stylish sailor fashions that complemented the Navy service issue during the War. Moore Haven's heyday had all the trappings of the "tin lizzie" society as well as the cowboys, farmers, and people who migrated to the town from other communities.

On the quiet street where Thelma lives not very far from her son, she welcomes visitors with the genuine charm and the graciousness of a true Southern lady. She reminds one of the warmth that has all but disappeared in the hurry and rush of life so prevalent in the bustling "things to do" neighborhoods. Although many tourists sometimes don't conceive of Florida as being a part of Southern culture, many pioneer families came from Georgia, Alabama, and the Carolinas. Titus Cook's parents came from Alabama; Thelma's from Texas. Many old southern traditions have become part of Florida's historical heritage.

Thelma and Tommy Cook enjoy telling the stories that they know first hand growing through the many stages of Moore Haven's changes. Passing through the old streets of the town square, walking along the grasspinched sidewalk to the hollow face of Lundy's Hardware dressed now with elongated vines clinging to its side, pausing in the shade of the ancient gigantic oak beside the river, one can enjoy the serenity that lured people to remain in this quiet remote section of Florida. The town square in Moore Haven hasn't changed a lot, except that every one of the original businesses is closed. Lundy's lasted the longest of the storefronts along the square, even into the 80's. Donald Lundy bought the mercantile store in 1974, long after it opened its doors as the Moore Haven Supply Company in 1915. But Lundy's was a store that had just about any kind of item needed to construct, rebuild, garden, or improvise. They also had the kind of people that could come up with an answer to almost any problem created by the unforgiving climate.

Tommy remembers spending long hours at the old pictures show, hanging out in the stores along the arcade that are all silent in repose, perhaps waiting for a rebirth in another time. Only the bank has been revived with much of its original structure preserved as the antique store filled with rich finds from area treasures.

A VISION OF MOORE HAVEN IN THE FUTURE

Although a huge concrete ceiling imposes the rumble of U.S. Highway traffic diverted overhead, it does not appear to disturb the laughter of children below playing in the park. Old Highway 27 used to cut through the small business community, but now the gigantic overpass cuts off the lifeblood of the city. Maybe the two story building and one room apartment that housed Thelma and their family above the bar in the old town square will once again welcome "ecotourists" as a bed and breakfast hotel. Maybe someone sailing along the river will recognize the solemn serenity of the little town and as the earlier developers envisioned a dream, someone new will follow in these footsteps and bring life to the sidewalks and music in the square along the river's shoulder. Maybe one day Moore Haven's web page will advertise to the world the unique cultural heritage of the town and attract tourists to explore the scenic life along Florida's old State Highways that lead into Moore Haven. Maybe Moore Haven's will once again awaken its economic potential and thrive on the heritage the town mirrors in the inner sanctum of cobwebbed ceilings, wooden floors and crusty storefronts that line the street of the one time commerce center of Glades County, restored to life as it once was in the 1900's. In 1995, Moore Haven Downtown Historic District was listed in the National Register of Historic Places.

Thelma Cook has been of a part of Moore Haven's history, she has seen the town thrive, subside and wane. But, it is the pioneering spirit of people like Thelma Cook that despite all of the trials and tribulations of Moore Haven, she has remained. Over the past 65 years, Thelma Cook still fondly calls Moore Haven her home.

AN OASIS IN THE PRAIRIE

The 1951 flood in Palmdale doesn't' keep the customers away for long at
the Oasis Bar and Grill

Since the 1930's and throughout the stormy dispute with Lykes Brothers in the 80's, another historic establishment in Palmdale, the Oasis Bar and Restaurant was the heartbeat of the town. The Oasis' legacy began in 1938 when the wife of railroad agent Ed Fleming opened the café. The yarns and episodes spun over drinks at the Oasis' wooden bar remain absorbed in rotting walls too far gone to be revived. The word-of-mouth epics of Palmdale's colorful life and personalities, subject of much elaboration, are now reminiscent memories. Clothes smelling of hamburger, home fries and horses, the jukebox whirling 45's blasting down the highway, and Minnie Mae's forever smile, is desperately solemn and silent. Frayed boards are slashed across the entrance and the lighted sign that once announced the sweet surrender of the Everglades inside the Oasis is now dark. The faded red shadow box sits like a coffin on a slab of cement awaiting burial. It was a cultural disaster when the historic Oasis closed its doors and another chapter in Palmdale's boom or bust history.

1999—The jukebox is silent at the red-matchbox Oasis Café deteriorating along U.S Highway 27 beneath the billboard of the last roadside attraction in Palmdale, Gatorama.

11

TEN-YEAR BATTLE TO SAVE FISHEATING CREEK

✦

1989–1999
PALMDALE

THE LIGHT OF DAY

A stilling breeze pierces the hollow silence, feathering through a thatch of palmettos spiking the crimson horizon of the morning sky. A dragon fly toe dances from one palmetto dagger to the other flashing a turquoise iridescence along its whimsical path. Sunlight streams shadows through the waving fans of a lone cabbage palm tracing its graceful stalk to the scrubs nestled below. Crickets and carpenter bees chatter in dissonant harmony, screeching crows announce their presence as the Glades awakens. The first light of day rises quickly, dissolving the night as if it never occurred.

In this tiny crevasse of the vast Everglades spectacle, a living image unfolds on Nature's palette that captures the senses and stamps its unique imprint upon space and time. There is a raw serenity here that tingles the spine and rekindles the spirit of the secret observer mingling in the shadows beneath the outstretched moss-laden arms of a solemn oak. And it is here, in the last wilderness area of Florida that the citizenry of a small town with undaunting courage and relentless spirit initiated a legal battle against a multi-international corporation to save Fisheating Creek as a public waterway. Palmdale, on the edge of the Everglade's prairie, a town of some 300 citizens took on Lykes Brothers.

PALMDALE VS MULTI-INTERNATIONAL LYKES BROTHERS, INC.

The property dispute between the State and Lykes Brothers had its roots in the 1980's. Lykes Brothers claimed that they, not the State, owned the portion of Fisheating Creek that ran through their property in Palmdale. A handful of 300 + determined Palmdale citizens challenged Lykes Brothers to preserve the heritage of Fisheating Creek as a navigable public waterway through their property.

In 1989, the battle between the people of Palmdale and Lykes Brothers peaked. For many years, Lykes Brothers allowed access to Fisheating Creek and several fishing holes on their Palmdale property. In 1989, Lykes barred public usage of the creek and posted inimical signs along the edge: "NO TRESPASSING. FISHEATING CREEK IS A NON-NAVIGABLE STREAM AND TRES-PASSERS WILL BE PROSECUTED, Lykes Brothers." Palmdale residents took their case to Attorney General Bob Butterworth.

In the meantime, as legal actions were pursued in the court, some restless Palm-dale residents pursued other "outlaw" measures. On Christmas Eve of 1989, Palmdale resident and descendant of pioneer ranchers, Lucky Whidden, boldly took an acetylene torch to the steel barricade Lykes Brothers posted as a barricade across the creek to block passage. In another incident, Smiley Hendry and his son were arrested for allegedly trespassing, cutting fences on Lykes property and assaulting a Lykes Brothers security guard. Becky Hendry (a Hendry County namesake), founder of "Sav the Creek, Inc." and wife of Smiley Hendry, refused any plea agreement from Lykes' attorney and insisted on going to trial or having all charges dropped. The charges were summarily dropped.

According to David Guest, formerly of the State Attorney General's office, employed by the Earth Justice Legal Defense Fund, the original lawsuit filed against Lykes Brothers in 1989 sought an injunction to immediately remove the posted signs on the creek that declared it was not a navigable waterway. Attorney General Bob Butterworth based the lawsuit upon the 1823 Florida Act declaring that all navigable rivers in Florida must remain forever public. Tampa Federal Court Judge Elizabeth Kovachevich dismissed this suit on September 22, 1989 ruling that there was "no jurisdiction" under the statute.

A second lawsuit filed by Attorney General Bob Butterworth was based upon the Rivers and Harbor Act of 1890 prohibiting activities that affect rivers without obtaining a permit from the Corps of Engineers. This suit was the result of Lykes allegedly felling trees across the creek to block passage on the stream. Tampa Judge Kovachevich again dismissed the suit and issued an opinion that it was up to the Corp of Engineers to determine if Fisheating Creek was a navigable waterway. Attorney General Bob Butterworth filed another lawsuit to demand a "navigability determination" on Fisheating Creek from the Corps of Engineers.

The dispute between Lykes Brothers and the State caused conflicting interests for the citizens of Palmdale. Some residents worked many years for Lykes Brothers and were afraid to jeopardize their livelihood, especially in a county that ranks near the highest in unemployment and near the lowest in per capita income in Florida. But the townspeople united, held meetings late into the night searching through old Florida books, memories, historic records and albums for hardcore evidence that Fishing Creek had been navigable as far back as the 1800's.

1800'S—BILLY BOWLEGS HUNTED GATORS IN THE CREEK

One old Florida book that turned up included a recorded account of Seminole Chief Billy Bowleg's gator hunting along Fisheating Creek in the 1800's. Chief Bowlegs (Cho-fee-hat-cho) spoke of paddling from Lake Okeechobee to camp at Palmdale, poling across Rainey Slough to the Peace River watershed and down the river to sell hides and obtain groceries. Also discovered in another existing journal was an account of an 1842 Naval expedition that traveled down Fisheating Creek in the dry season in twelve, 30-foot canoes with sail and rudder. These historical records provided additional evidence in the case supporting the navigability of Fisheating Creek.

Ancestral Florida Indians the Calusas, the Yemasees, and "Mikasukees" called Fisheating Creek, "Tlalklapopka-hatchee." Early Seminole Indians (a Creek word for runaways) used the Creek as an escape route from the U.S. troops during the Seminole wars in the 1800's. Rock slabs in Fisheating Creek near Lakeport are the remains of Ft. Center where Seminoles were captured for bounty after the war. Homesteading pioneers depended on the Creek for transportation, trading and a mail route to other towns sprouting up on the inland waterway.

On Feb. 1, 1990, the Corps of Engineers issued its findings: Fisheating Creek was navigable. Following the release of the report, an attempt to attain Lykes Brothers concurrence that Fisheating Creek was a public river was unsuccessful.

In April, 1990, Lykes took the Corps to court. Two years later, July, 1992, Judge Kovachevich set a bench trial in Ft. Myers that coursed the summer of 1992. At the end, Judge Kovachevich issued a post-trial memorandum, ruling that even though a dugout canoe could cross from Okeechobee to Palmdale, it did not prove that the stream was "navigable." In September 1993, a fourth suit was filed based upon the river being publicly owned under State law. The trial was set for April 22, 1997.

A QUESTIONABLE VICTORY

On June 2, 1997, after a six-week jury trial under Circuit Court Judge Charles T. Carlton, a verdict was returned in 1-½ hours, ruling that Fisheating Creek was indeed a navigable waterway belonging to the State. In Dec. 3, 1999, the case was settled.

Represented by Florida Attorney General, Bob Butterworth, the Earth Justice Defense Fund, The Environmental Confederation of Southwest Florida and "Sav the Creek, Inc.," the town won a lawsuit and property settlement agreement against Lykes Brothers, one of the largest property owners in Glades County, a international shipping magnate, citrus king and pioneer cattle barons. The settlement agreement was finalized December 3, 1999 after a ten-year legal harangue that established a wilderness area of more than 42,000 acres along historic Fisheating Creek flowing through the heart of Palmdale and Lykes Brothers property. Lykes brothers own approximately 82% of Glades County, which ranks near the bottom of per capita income in the state and near the top of unemployment in the State.

The State of Florida paid $46 million to Lykes Brothers for property on, and surrounding Fisheating Creek designated as a Wildlife Management Area. Lykes Brothers abandoned their claim to 9,000 acres of State owned land on the Creek. The State purchased an extended corridor of another 9,000 acres adjacent to the riverbed for designated recreational use and 42,000 acres (eventually 120 thousand acres) for a conservation easement to be maintained as an environmentally protected area.

1999—Fisheating Creek opens to the public under the Florida Fish and
Wildlife Conservation Commission

The new area was reserved for primitive camping, hunting (in specific locations/
seasons) and canoeing along 23 miles of Fisheating Creek that snakes through
native Cypress Swamp. The former Lykes Brothers Campground and popular
swimming hole of Palmdale residents was established as part of the concession
area on the west side of U.S. 27 with several access areas to the Creek off Palmdale's Main Street, according to Monica Reimer of the State Attorney General's
office.

However, there was one hitch in the settlement agreement. Tom Gaskins, Sr.,
who founded the Cypress Knee Museum along former State Road 25 (now
Highway 27) in the 1930s, formerly owned by Lykes Brothers now belonged to
the State. Tom Gaskins, Sr. and his then young family, lived on the Lykes owned
land since the 1930's based upon a hand-shake agreement between Tom Gaskins,
Sr. and Charlie Lykes, Sr., one of the original seven Lykes brothers. The proof of
a legal written deed entitling Gaskins Jr. and family to remain on the home-
steaded property after Gaskins, Sr. and Lykes, Sr. passed away could not be established or secured. Tom Gaskins's livelihood, the historic workshop and home was
threatened by the events that occurred when Lykes Brothers' decided to shut
down Fisheating Creek.

Scattered cypress knees line the entrance to the Cypress Knee Workshop
in Palmdale

According to Tom Gaskins, Jr., the hand-built cypress tree residence of Tom
Gaskins, Sr., the cypress knee workshop, and the unique hand built cabbage palm
home would have to be relocated as well as his family, either across U.S. 27 next
to the Museum that Gaskins owns, or to his other property in Tasmania, ten
miles north. However, the Settlement Agreement between Lykes, the State and
Gaskins threw out the question of who owns the hand made cypress structures on
the property?

Part of the State's settlement, claimed sections of Lykes Brothers property on
both sides of U.S 27, including the residential homestead of the deceased Tom
Gaskins, Sr. on the East Side of the highway, across from the Cypress Knee
Museum he founded in the 1930's. When State Road 25 became U.S. 27, the
property where Gaskins Sr. lived was split down the middle. The Cypress Knee
Museum was located on the west side of the highway; the residence built by Tom
Gaskins, Sr., the cypress knee workshop/catwalk, and the cabbage palm residence
built by Gaskins, Jr. was east of U.S. 27.

Uncut cypress knees left unsculptured at the close of the Cypress Knee Workshop

The hand-built cypress tree home of the Tom Gaskins, Jr. family Palmdale

EVICTED

On November 4, 1999, Lykes Brothers, on behalf of the State of Florida, ordered Tom Gaskins Jr. to vacate the property by December 3, 1999, the closing date of the property settlement; Gaskins did not vacate. On February 16, 2000, an "Eviction Notice" was filed by Lykes in Glades County Court. The Complaint stated that Lykes was withholding their consent for continued possession of the property effective December 3, 1999.

On May 3, 2000, a motion to transfer the "Eviction Notice" case to Hendry County was granted by Judge Keith Cary who scheduled a jury trial in his court June 7, 2000. The complaint, filed by Lykes Brothers, delineated an action to recover possession of unlawfully detained real property located in Glades County, Florida under Section 8201 of the Florida Statute. The complaint asked for damages (back rent) and possession of the property. The complaint stated that Gaskins Jr. did not pay any rent on the property while living there since the 1930's.

Tom Gaskins, Jr. said there was a boundary dispute and attempted to negotiate a land trade with Lykes and the State to remain on the property. The regional Historical Society recommended to the State that the Gaskins' homestead be registered as a National Historic Site. However, Tom Gaskins, Jr., whose wife had been diagnosed with cancer and undergone two major surgeries, wanted to resolve the conflict as quickly as possible. In lieu of a trial, he said he would relocate the historical residence to his property in Venus (Tasmania). The historic 1930's homestead of pioneer Tom Gaskins Sr., the Cypress Knee workshop and cabbage palm residence of Tom Gaskins, Jr. was about to become another disembodied landmark in Palmdale's ragged history.

THE FATE OF A PIONEER HOMESTEAD

"The Agreed Final Judgment" on two, of three remaining lawsuits by Lykes Brothers against Tom Gaskins, Jr. that relinquished all rights, title and interest or claim to the real property upon which the Tom Gaskins, Jr. family has been residing for more than forty years, was settled. Lykes brothers conveyed the land to the State of Florida December 2, 1999 subject to the contractual duty of Lykes to clear title and deliver possession of the land to the state. When Tom Gaskins, Jr. did not vacate the property by the closing date of the Lykes/State of Florida property settlement agreement, an eviction notice was filed by Lykes in Glades County, and then moved to Hendry County, for a jury trial originally scheduled for June 7. However, in lieu of the mediation to negotiate an agreement that was ongoing between Lykes attorney, Bert Harris, Gaskins Attorney Kenneth Jones, a Mediator and The Nature's Conservancy, a non-profit organization, the trial was postponed. The last remaining unsettled lawsuit that attorneys refrained from providing details, involved the Cypress Knee Museum property on the west side of U.S. 27, across from the Gaskins homestead.

The "Agreed Final Judgment" delineated that the "personal property and improvements situated on the land (including all buildings and their respective contents, but excluding all trees and growing things) are the property of Tom Gaskins Jr. and Billie Jo Gaskins, husband and wife. Plaintiff Lykes makes no claim upon Gaskins' personal property. Lykes waived and relinquished all claims for rents, profits, and damages against Gaskins pertaining to the Gaskins' use and occupation of the land. Defendants Gaskins shall file for any and all variances needed to utilize their Venus (Tasmania) property for the Gaskins personal property on or before June 9, 2000. Should it be necessary for the variance request to be considered and decided by the County Commission, the Gaskins' shall diligently pursue such application so as to have the variance request scheduled at the first legally available County Commission meeting. The Gaskins' shall remove the Gaskins' personal property from the land within 90 days of the final administrative decision on the variance by the Planning and Zoning Commission or the County Commission, whether such decision be a granting or denial of the variance. Any portion of the Gaskins' personal property remaining on the land after the above deadline shall be deemed abandoned by the Gaskins and shall become the property of the State without further action, order of judgment." The judgment was approved and agreed upon by all parties, and filed in Hendry County June 8, 2000.

Attached to the "Agreed Final Judgment" was the "Mediation Agreement." Attorney James Nulman acted as the mediator between Lykes Brothers and the Gaskins family with all parties meeting in Ft. Myers, June 2nd, 2000. The mediation agreement involved the relocation of Gaskins personal property (all buildings and contents) to Tasmania part of Venus, north of Palmdale off U.S. Highway 27. An additional clause in the Mediation Agreement stated: "Should it be necessary for the variance request to be considered, Lykes hereby agrees that neither Lykes, nor any Officer, Director, employee, or representative of Lykes, shall in any way oppose or object to Gaskins' application(s) for such variance(s) to utilize the Venus (Tasmania) property."

Further stipulations of the Agreement: "Lykes is entitled to entry of the "Agreed Final Judgment" upon proof that $75,000.00 to be paid by the Nature Conservancy into Gaskins' Attorney, Ken Jones Trust Account. The parties agree to equally divide and pay the Mediator's Fees, one half being paid by Gaskins and one-half by Lykes. A counterclaim by Tom Gaskins and Billie Jo Gaskins was dismissed against Plaintiff Lykes, with prejudice."

"The Nature Conservancy will pay $75,000 towards the cost of moving the Gaskins' personal property from the land to the Venus (Tasmania) area in Glades County. The escrow agent, Attorney Ken Jones will disburse the trust funds to the vendors relocating the Gaskins' personal property upon written certification by The Nature Conservancy that the expenses related to moving Gaskins are approved. The trust funds shall be used exclusively to move the Gaskins personal property to Venus (Tasmania) or such other property as the Gaskins' select in the event the permits and variances are not obtained for the Venus (Tasmania) property. Such expense includes such items as, but is not limited to, permits, variances, infrastructure, moving the structures and other personal property. Any funds remaining in the trust account not utilized for authorized relocation expenses shall be repaid to The Nature Conservancy."

Elthea Stafford, Director of Glades County Planning and Zoning Department indicated that the removal of the personal property of Tom Gaskins' homestead (the cabbage palm residence of Tom and Billie Jo Gaskins, the cypress knee Workshop and original hand built Cypress home of now deceased pioneer Tom Gaskins, Sr.) fell under the "Family Homestead" guidance law meaning Gaskins did not have to apply for any variances from the County Commission or the Planning and Zoning Department in order to re-locate his belongings to his property in Tasmania.

Ms. Stafford outlined the stipulations of the Building and Zoning Codes and explained that the Family Homestead law allows Gaskins to move the property to the new location, but forever after, he cannot sell any of the property to anyone other than a family member. Gaskins only needed to apply for the appropriate permits, and complete all requirements prior to the permits being obtained. After permits are obtained with construction drawings completed, and inspections authorized, then the power could be turned on at the new location. According to Brian Prowant, Environmental Specialist with the Glades County Health Department, the clock started ticking June 9th, on the 90 day removal period of the personal property, the date he issued the septic tank permit for the new location.

THE FINAL DAYS OF 1999

The Gaskins' family had already begun to pack up the Cypress Knee Workshop piece by piece on pick-up trucks, until the final day when the huge caravan of 1930's historic residential structures would travel down U.S. highway 27 to its final destination in Tasmania.

Evicted! Palmdale's historical Cypress Knee workshop is loaded onto trucks

After forty-years where three generations of Gaskins' lived, all that is left behind is the old plank boardwalk circling the swamp where the 50-year-old cypress knee sculptures will be taken back into the Everglades. Coke bottles sucked into the bark of the growing knees will never be seen again. And the sour orange tree that Tom Gaskins' Sr. used to tout to the tourists was "the sweetest orange in Glades County," would stand-alone in the vacant spot that used to guard the entrance to the workshop. Tourists can still remember the laugh as they took a bite out of the bitterest native orange they ever tasted. The personality of the man, the Museum, and the art will soon disappear forever from this homestead.

Larry Campbell, of the Division of Fish and Wildlife Conservation Commission, the agency designated as the managers of the new Management Area was asked if there were any plans for the State to construct another catwalk, or other structures on the Gaskins homestead property when vacated, but he said there were no plans. Today, the property is encased in a steel fence and the two-planked catwalk is being taken back by the swamp.

2000—THE GASKINS' HOMESTEAD LOADED ON FLAT BED TRUCKS

As the nation celebrated its birth on July 4th, 2000, the Tom Gaskins' family prepared to move Palmdale's historical landmark, the 1930's homestead of Florida pioneer Tom Gaskins, Sr.'s handmade Cypress workshop, residence and Gaskins, Jr.'s cabbage palm structured house to Tasmania, near Venus.

In the pictorial display in the center of the book, Tom Gaskins, Jr. described, in his own words, "a soon to be lost art." "My personal feelings are one thing and having lived with this place (the Cypress Knee Museum and homestead established by Tom Gaskins, Sr. in 1937) for 59 of the 64 years it has been here, puts it close to my heart. My personal feelings aside, to see a place as true and genuine to old Florida ripped to shreds by the State that just twelve years ago conferred upon it the 1987 "Heritage Award," tells me that the left hand doesn't know what the right hand is doing in Tallahassee. Governor Bush could have solved this problem, and he knows about it full well. But he chose to remain aloof. If you ask me, it was insane to do this.'

"My father developed many skills sculpturing Florida cypress knees that he passed down to me and I was beginning to pass on to my sons when Lykes Brothers cut us off from cutting Cypress knees ten to twelve years ago. At one time, it was a very happy arrangement, but new people came on the scene and things changed."

Billie Jo expressed her appreciation for all of the support friends have given the family, in letters, faxes and kind notes. Billie Jo, who survived breast cancer surgery during the ordeal, conveyed a gracious and generous smile as she expressed her gratitude "I can't put into words how much I appreciate the barbecue benefit at Hendry's Sabal Palm Campground, and all of the people who came out to offer the family support all the way from Palmdale to Tallahassee." Billie Jo said they were ready "to move forward with their lives, but is sad thinking about what the State and Lykes Brothers have done do the historical site." The homestead, when re-located to Tasmania will not be open to the public.

THE MAN WHO WORE NO SHOES

The life of Tom Gaskins Sr., the founder of the Cypress Knee Museum, embraces the true Florida "cracker" spirit. In the early 1900's, Tom Gaskins, Sr. and his son passed through Palmdale from Arcadia and often stayed at the Palmdale Hotel. In 1937, he settled in Palmdale and began a mail-order business selling hand made turkey callers and cypress knees. He cut, skinned and sold the cypress knees to taxidermists for mounting everything from birds to bears. For $1.00, he invited tourists to visit the Museum and take a daring catwalk that still swings precariously from cypress trees above the swamp behind the workshop on the East side of U.S. 27. He enjoyed the look on visitors' faces, including the author's, when he offered a taste of a wild (bitter) Florida orange from the tree outside the workshop.

"Tom Gaskins, Sr. the original founder of the Cypress Knee Museum at Palmdale was born in Tampa, March 26, 1909. He was raised in Arcadia and graduated with the Class of 1927. He worked with and was a salesman for Gator Roach killer until 1934 when he married Virginia Bible and started the cypress knee industry. In 1937, they moved to Palmdale where they lived in a house covered with about 30,000 hand-split cypress shingles, every one he made. In 1947, he invented, manufactured and started selling his unique and nationally famous wild turkey callers. The Cypress Knee Museum opened in 1951. At age 69, he still jogged eleven miles, barefoot, everyday through the cypress knee swamp along Fisheating Creek, near the old Moore Haven road grade behind his house. Gaskins, Sr. called himself a woodsman, hunter, fisherman, and woodcarver. He held ten patents for inventions during his lifetime" (*Florida Facts and Fallacies, by Tom Gaskins,* 1978).

Tom Gaskins, Sr. established his Museum on the Tin Lizzie Trail to Palmdale, when old model-T's took "a day or two to travel 50 miles but it was faster than horse or horse and wagon." Since there were no motels in Florida's early days, people pitched a camp on what was called "pine islands" or high ground, although by the 70's Gaskins claims that much of the water was drained, leaving armadillos and ditches. Gaskins' book, publishes many "Florida cracker" wisdoms, a term he declares has a debatable origin. Either the Florida cracker gained reputation from the cow hunter's quick crack of their whip, or from a North/South battle in North Florida when crack shots were credited to Florida Crackers. Today, a "Florida Cracker" is referred to as a Native, born and raised in the State.

The Everglades, since time memorial is identified with the jagged-edged saw grass and the cypress tree. Cypress trees generally grow in low areas where there is a lot off water. Cypress trees that string out over miles, is called a "cypress strand." Behind the Gaskins' residence was a vast cypress swamp with long cypress strands that still exists today in Palmdale providing a shaded canopy along Fisheating Creek.

According to Gaskins, Sr. "the only tree that has knees is cypress, but all cypress do not have knees. Cypress knees grow up from the roots of the tree and have no leaves, no limbs, and they do not make a tree. Gaskins thought knees stored water for the tree during dry weather, or to aerate roots of the tree during high water, or were an evolutionary left-over when it was a protective device like a thorn." The theory best liked by pioneer Gaskins was "one supplied by a visitor, toothpicks for dinosaurs!"

The sculptured cypress knees are natural, but undergo a simple process invented by Gaskins, Sr. to enhance its beauty. Normally cypress knees are solid. When Gaskins began to cut and peel them he saw the opportunity to make things out of them and sell them. He first advertised cypress knees in House and Gardens

Magazine in November 1935. He has a patent on the manufacturing of them since 1937.

At the Cypress Knee Museum, he had a collection of knees from twenty-three states in a vast variety of forms. Usually the knees grow up straight, but then Nature becomes creative. In the museum, Gaskins had one called a "Lady Hippo-potamus Wearing a Carmen Miranda Hat." One last walk through the cypress swamp, along the hand-made catwalk behind the cypress knee workshop, the progress over twenty years of natural growth, evolved a different and unique sculptor from the original description carved on the sign, posted on the earlier date, soon to be taken back by the encroaching Everglades habitat when left on its own.

What will not disappear is the original craft passed down by apprenticeship from Gaskins, Sr. to Gaskins, Jr. and his sons: The sculpturing of the raw cypress knees into objects of art. The process is long and precise. The tools often hand-crafted by Gaskins, Sr. from everyday utensils. The old chair, which became a part of

Gaskins Sr.'s life for more two-thirds of a century remains, and one can feel the frame of the man molded into the back of the two cypress limbs where the sculptor spent his life working with nature's mysterious cypress knees and artistic imagination to create lamps, tables, mounts for birds and bears for all those who passed through the portals of his workshop. The woven lampshades, hand made from palms, the polished statutes, some hovering over five feet, lined the workshop in various stages of completion.

Before the flat bed trucks arrived to carry them into an unknown future, the wooden floors were scattered with pieces of knees. If the art will be revived is not known, but the skill of the unique craft will forever be the inheritance of Tom Gaskins Jr. and his two sons, Tom III, and Jim.

2004: THE EVERGLADES RECLAIMS ITS OWN

The State erected a fence around the property where Tom Gaskins' used to take his daily barefoot run in the swamp, crossing the old railroad bed that one time carried cypress trees to the lumber mill. That too is only a rusted, overgrown memory. There is no monument from the lives carved out of the cypress forest. Even the old Museum across the road is sinking into the sand, unattended and uncared for. A legacy has disappeared in Palmdale and only those who watched Tom Gaskins and his sons carve the clocks, the lamps and turkey whistles will remember what used to be, every time that empty spot is passed along the highway. Nature left the old sour orange tree to stand guard by the limestone path that carried millions of footsteps into the wilderness.

Photo: *Courtesy of Bud Adams, The Adams Ranch, Ft. Pierce, Florida*

12

THE CREEK IS MANAGED

✦

2000

As part of the December, 1999 "Settlement Agreement" between the State of Florida and Lykes Brothers which opened up more than 23 miles of Fisheating Creek and its corridors as a conservation area for public use, the Fish and Wildlife Conservation Commission were assigned by the Board of Trustees as joint managers.

Traveling south from Okeechobee along State Road 78, one passes through a time capsule of Florida history from the sprawling ranch prairies to the marsh area west of the dike past Buckhead Ridge, Lightsey's restaurant (one of the best) to the welcoming sign of Lakeport just inside Glades County. At least one time or another, travelers have stopped in for supplies and a visit with long time resident and proprietor Lewis Collins. Collins runs the store, his mother the two pump gas station next door. Both have long memories of the early banana grove, planted by step-aunt Lelia Platt along the twisting curves of Fisheating Creek. This area was planned to be a unique nature walk for people to participate in the natural wilderness experience (2004—the nature walk has not been constructed).

Wildlife Biologist, Grant Steelman, who was appointed to manage the natural wildlife communities, expresses a deep charisma with the vegetative and animal habitats along the corridors of Cow Bone Marsh, the cypress strands and oak hammocks where "silence" is a rare commodity for miles shared only with the stillness of the wildlife secretly observing the human intruders. This area, however, was prohibited to the public until the Conservation Area was established by the Settlement Agreement with the State and Lykes.

119

Steelman easily is a part of this natural world, as his trained eye observes minute details of pickerel weed, fire flags and cypress seed pods that provide food for many of the vegetarian species rooting in the deep grass along their hunting trail.

Along parts of the 23 miles of Fisheating Creek that is open to the public for primitive camping, canoeing, fishing hunting and airboat enthusiasts, a joint co-existent plan was worked out by the Fish and Wildlife Conservation Commission to participate in various interests, designating locations and seasons for hunting and air boating. The Commission delineated six square miles off State Road 78, at the Fisheating Creek oxbow, a few miles adjacent to the unprotected Ft. Center Indian Mounds, for airboat recreation with permits. The Commission announced that they were striving to provide opportunities for everyone to have access to the Creek and enjoy the surrounding wilderness while preserving the pristine serenity and natural unspoiled beauty.

By 2000, Steelman envisioned educational youth program to explore the habitat along Fisheating Creek, the behaviors of alligators, wild boar, black bear and Florida panther (a rarely sighted indigenous to the area). Families of wild boar and black bears are frequent visitors. Steelman said that recently a lone Florida panther had been spotted camping along the Creek, but to his disappointment, the panther was later found dead from undetermined causes.

With the heightened interest of visitors returning to winter along Fisheating Creek, Steelman holds a Masters Degree and can offer an accountability of the natural surroundings. He expresses a genuine interest in learning as much as possible about his assigned area that is similar in habitat to the Big Cypress Swamp, his former tour of duty.

One Lakeport pioneer that is accessible to the public is Luke Collins who runs the store and "filling station" on State Road 78. Steelman considers Lewis Collins as his best source of information due to the family's own long history in the area. If not leaning over a book behind the cash register, Lewis Collins knows about Ft. Center (marking the site of the Indian mounds across Fisheating Creek oxbow) and used to hunt wild hogs around the site many years ago. Soldiers at the fort were part of the move to rid Florida of the Indians during the Indian Wars. Many Indians were captured and mercilessly sold by soldiers for bounty.

Rising over the deep ditches along the Creek one can imagine from primitive maps, a lookout area that could easily have been the site of the Fort. The rock slabs, the last alleged remains of the Fort, that are said to lie at the bottom of the Creek could not be located on a winding search along the creek bed. However, the excavation site of the Indian mound is still prevalent, and a fascinating aerial photo Steelman researched, compared with old maps reveals the possible site of old Indian burial grounds. In 1962, when Lykes owned the land, an archeologist Dr. William Sears speculated that the mounds were occupied before the time of Christ until about 1000 A.D.

Lakeport is a small remote town with a few surrounding houses, a motel, restaurants and trailer parks. There is still wildlife in the less populated area and Steelman, who is housed at Lakeport, studies and tracks the animals. Steelman says the wild boars that hang out at the marshes usually "root" in the wee hours and keep their distance from people, unless cornered. There are still plentiful deer in the Cow Bone Marsh area at the oxbow and can often be seen fleeting into the brush. Steelman says on walks back into the marsh he has seen flocks of swallowtail kites soaring overhead into tall willow trees or Australian pines. Steelman had plans to reestablish indigenous plants and provide food to attract wildlife to the protected area.

One tip Steelman emphasizes to visitors to the Conservation area is to avoid feeding any of the wildlife, especially the alligators and boars. Feeding wildlife disrupts their natural food chain sources and can create problems for humans by drawing a wild animal closer to human habitat.

Boars and deer are the most prevalent of the larger mammals in the marsh community. Although Steelman said that the natural habitat of the Black Bear is characteristic of the Cypress thicket is seldom spotted in the Fisheating Creek area, and if is present it usually stays undercover. However, a Bear is an "animal of opportunity", and if campers leave out dog food, or any source of food, it can attract any animal. Steelman added that there are no recorded unprovoked attacks by Black Bears in Florida.

Steelman says that Black Bears are very rare although on U.S. 27 north of Palmdale there are signs cautioning motorists of Florida Black Bear crossings. Unlike the bear's northern relatives, it does not hibernate. The female adults weigh about two to three hundred pounds, with one to three cubs per year, and the male weighs in at about 600 pounds. In the state, there is an estimated 3 to 5,000 Black Bears in various sections of Florida. With all wild animals, Steelman says that they will usually retreat if a human approaches. Aggressive behavior by any of the wildlife is usually "provoked" by someone attempting to hand feed or take a picture at too close range of an animal. But most animals are afraid of the human species, just as much as the human species is leery of the wildlife.

In 1999, as the first Wildlife Biologist for the new Management Area, Steelman said his focus was on managing habitat for wildlife conservation and recreation. He said he would work in concert with the Commission to design control plans for "exotics," species not indigenous to Florida. The Commission planned to employ mechanical and vegetation control with prescribed burns, to restore and maintain natural habitat. Steelman stressed that the Commission's goal was to provide the most opportunity for everyone to enjoy the natural setting.

Prior to the Settlement Agreement, the public was restricted from the area for many years, as it was privately owned by Lykes Brothers. In 2004, sportsmen can hunt in specified areas with permits in set-aside seasons without charge (unless for "special opportunity" hunts), others can canoe and camp along the corridors of the Creek in areas that were previously not available. The Florida Fish and Wildlife Commission state that their Mission is to offer the public the greatest enjoyment of the land.

In 1999, the Commission announced a "special opportunity turkey" hunt east of U.S. 27, for the Fall. The Commission also publishes a "Regulations Summary and Area Map" pamphlet available at the Lakeport Store.

THE EFFORT CONTINUES

The small community of Palmdale began the initiative in the 1980's to "Sav the Creek," with Becky Hendry heading up the legal battle. Twenty years late, after ten years of lawsuits were resolved, and the land returned to the public, the public still has limited access to the cordoned off areas.

The new Conservation Management area has limitless opportunities to provide a wilderness experience for young and old, hunter, camper, canoeists, hiker, bicyclist, and for those who just want to commune with Nature in serene silence.

What is unique about the new caretakers of the land, the Fish and Wildlife Conservation Commission is their management practices. They espoused a commitment to provide more opportunities for visitors than if the area was operated as a State Park (state parks prohibits many of the activities that the Commission allows).

By 2004, the hand-made catwalk cutting through the cypress forest on the former property of Tom Gaskins in Palmdale is fenced by the State and overgrown. It has been closed to the public since the 1999 agreement with the State and Lykes Brothers was finalized. The site of the former Cypress Knee workshop was originally proposed to be re-vitalized and a new boardwalk constructed and open to the public. The swamp has reinstated its domain.

1999 WILDLIFE MANAGEMENT UPDATE ON THE CREEK:

NEW REGULATIONS AND PHASED DEVELOPMENT OF THE WILDLIFE MANAGEMENT AREA FROM THE FISH AND WILDLIFE CONSERVATION COMMISSION

Larry Campbell, of the Fish and Wildlife Conservation Commission, heads the agency assigned as jointed managers with the Board of Trustees of the State of Florida, to oversee the more than 60 thousand conservation acres along Fisheating Creek and its corridors. Campbell said the agency was moving ahead with "new venues on several fronts" to fulfill the Property Settlement Agreement finalized in December 1999 between Lykes Brothers and the State of Florida. The management plans involved several phases.

PALMDALE CAMPSITE—WEST OF U.S. 27

On June 15th, 2000 the agency opened bids for the operation of the old Lykes Brothers campground in Palmdale that although was expected to be completed by July 1, did not open until a year later. The concession, on the west side of U.S. 27 was initially opened as a day use area (7 a.m. to dark) for overnight primitive camping/canoeing with vehicles allowed to park outside the entrance gate just across the railroad tracks, about 1/4 mile from the Creek. A sign was posted prohibiting vehicles from remaining on the campsites after dark.

Larry Campbell, Wildlife Commission Director, said the restrictions were put into place to maintain a family oriented campground and prevent continuous vandalism to the buildings and bathrooms on the property. One camper at the Palmdale site, Arlene Byrd of LaBelle who was there for three days with her three children said "that if the kids get hurt, or if a wild boar should come around, or another emergency occur the distance to the car, when seconds count, could be critical." A roving Wildlife Conservation Officer had been ticketing people with a $50.00 fine if they did not relocate their vehicles from the camping site after dark.

The larger parking area located inside the fence, initially was not open for parking. Campbell said there may be some relaxation of the regulations after a live-on-the property supervisor is hired. Campbell said, "There is no stipulation in the Settlement Agreement that prevents a live-on-site supervisor" (when the campground opened the new leasing agents lived on site).

Another regulation regarding leashed dogs on the campsites and the miles of hiking/walking/jogging trails that other State parks permit (Jonathan Dickinson and Babcock Park near Punta Gorda, the latter managed by the same agency) was said by Campbell to be restricted. However, according to the Attorney General's Office, there is no stipulation in the Settlement Agreement that restricts leashed dogs in the camp area, or on the hiking trails. The only prohibition is on hunting dogs in the campground.

"Buck" enjoys the shade of an oak tree at the Creek

Additionally, the double Olympic size pond, on the north side of the campground was cleared of alligators and planned to be re-opened for swimming.

The State budgeted funds for improvements on Fisheating Creek, provided for an engineering firm on the site after July 1st, to evaluate the sewer and water treatment plant; an electrician to update and repair power lines and buildings.

ACCESS AREAS TO FISHEATING CREEK:

<u>Main Street in Palmdale</u>: Vehicles are not allowed on the old grade to protect the natural environment from swamp buggies and other all terrain vehicles, but canoes can be carried from Main Street and put in at the Creek. Fishing and primitive camping are allowed. A new fence line is in place near Lucky Whidden's house (burned down in 2002) and to the access point at Main Street and on areas both east and west of U.S. 27.

HUNTING:

The first applications for hunting permits closed June 12th. Those that did file for a permit were to be chosen on a lottery basis; 20 permits were available for deer and hogs. If an Alligator hunting season would be established was not yet determined. Hunting is permitted west of U. S. 27 except for a "special opportunity" turkey hunt in the spring. Hunting near the west side campground is restricted to a perimeter to be determined.

The following hunting dates have been established:

September 15–17	Archery Hunt	Deer/Hogs
September 22–24	Archery Hunt	Deer/Hogs
October 13–25 and	Muzzle Loading Guns	Deer/Hogs
October 20–22		
November 3–5 and		
November 24–26	General Gun Hunt	Deer/Hogs
December 9–10	General Gun Hunt	Hogs Only
		(5 permits)

The amount of game allowed during designated hunting days: One hog per day; one deer; turkeys—1 per permit; gray squirrels—2.

ADDITIONAL IMPROVEMENTS UNDERWAY IN 1999:

Creek maintenance: A contract has been let for a company to keep the Creek cleared for canoes; The Department of Environmental Protection and the Corps of Engineers is initiating control of exotic vegetation, Mallaluca trees and non-native species. A plan for the best management practices to protect the natural resources is being worked out with Lykes Brothers who are allowed to graze cattle in the Creek.

Road work: Roads were scheduled for repair off State Road 74 at Burnt Bridge and at Ingram's Crossing on the Tasmania grade near State Road 74 to Venus.

According to Campbell, further management plans on the Creek would be initiated in accordance with the settlement agreement.

DATELINE 1999: RE-OPENING THE PALMDALE CAMPGROUND

From the Fish and Wildlife Conservation Commission: Director Larry Campbell reports that one applicant was being reviewed for the Concessionaire at the Palmdale Campground with an anticipated opening by August after all inspections and refurbishing of facilities is completed. Part of the criteria for receiving the concession, includes providing scheduled canoe trips, including one guided by a naturalist, starting at Burnt Bridge and Ingram's Crossing back to the campsite. Some of the canoe trips will be overnight, with camping along the Creek. Campbell says the emphasis on the campsite operation is a family oriented place where hiking trails, fishing and the enjoyment of a natural wilderness experience are foremost.

The campground offers a pristine quiet in which to enjoy the sounds of birds, with cool winds gently cavorting through the canopy of oaks that shade the sun. At the campground fish can be seen leaping across the dark tannic waters of Fisheating Creek. Campbell says the small family of wild boars is not a threat to visitors.

STARGAZING PALMDALE: *"NO LIGHT POLLUTION"*

The wonder of gazing into a canopy of stars on a pitch-black night beckons astronomers, astrologers, amateur scientists, and dreamers. Stargazing has been a practice of the ancients who used primitive instruments and their imagination to outline the mythological images of Orion, Copernicus, and numerous other characterizations sprinkled in stardust throughout the heavens. Galileo, who is credited with the invention of the telescope, understood little, at first, about the grand spectacle that blanketed the ceiling of the Earth. Solemn observers aimed their instruments into the darkness creating stories, predictions and tales that made the night sky come alive.

Since the dawning of man and the evolution of civilization, the young Earth's skies began to fade into an aura of city lights casting an eerie glow miles away on an earthly scale on dark lonely highway. As civilization continued to spiral through once wilderness areas, bright artificial lights of sprawling cities reached into space and were captured in the shutter of satellite imagery. Manmade lights are a byproduct of urban growth. However, there is still one place on Earth where the skies are pristine, dark as ink and the stars shine in their brightest elegance. To appreciate the naked night sky in its raw beauty, one does not need to travel far, just to Palmdale where stargazers can share their curiosity and interest in learning about the celestial objects.

Mary and Dow Roland are wilderness guides who provide Everglades expeditions, swamp walks, tropical boat cruises and tours. Mary Roland's interests span the natural world of medicine, native plants, and shell collecting as well as taking the helm of a boat as Captain. The Roland's, both Native Floridians, have led tours through coastal barrier islands, tropical hardwood hammocks and will be guiding tours through Fisheating Creek. Dow Roland's interest is in tropical plants, bird watching archeology, paleontology, wildlife photography and Florida history.

One of the Roland's favorite spots is Palmdale where they explore their interests in nature and the wilderness of Fisheating Creek. In the month of November, Mary Roland initiated a new project at the campground called "Connect with the Spirit of the Night Skies." At sunset, Saturday, November 14 and November 24, Mary and Dow Roland brought out their telescope, inflatable lounge chairs, comforters, pillows and hot coffee along with visitors to share their knowledge of the constellations, a group of stars based upon Greek mythology that form a picture in the night sky.

The November star party featured the rise of the Goddess of Love, Venus, and the largest planet that gracefully lifts her head on the last rays of sunset in the western sky. Between November through March of 1999, Venus was at the height of her brightness since 1992. Mary and Dow Roland viewed the Orion Constellation and the Orion Nebulae, the cloudy birthplace of stars. Mary said, "within the Nebulae there are three stars in a straight line and at a right angle, a group of faint stars that form Orion's sword hanging from his giant belt. Orion, the Hunter in the eastern sky was said to be arrogant and boasted that there was nothing he could not shoot or any animal that could defeat him. The Mother Goddess sent Scorpius, the fatal scorpion, from the western sky to punish Orion for his arrogance. Orion died and the punishment for his behavior was that his image would be forever embedded in the night sky. Orion is seen setting into the underworld as the Scorpion rises" (www.einstein.stcloudstate.edu). These famous mythological characters are part of the constellations that have been classified over the past 6,000 years. On a dark night, about 1,000 to 1,500 stars can be seen at Palmdale; constellations help stargazers identify and remember star groups.

The Greeks recognized and named forty-eight constellations. Twelve constellations lie on the ecliptic and are known as "the Zodiacs." The names of the constellations are in Latin the language of learning. The ancients named the constellations after certain images the star formations seemed to outline in the sky. For thousands of years, people have used their knowledge of the constellations to guide them from place to place. Knowing the positions of the constellations, it is possible to locate other stars, planets, comets and meteors. The constellations appear to move westward as the Earth rotates around this sun. For this reason, certain constellations can be seen only during one of the seasons of the year. Some historians suspect that many of the myths associated with constellations such as Scorpius were invented to help farmers know the season to plant or harvest crops although constellations have changed over time.

In the technological age, constellations have been redefined so that every star in the sky is in exactly one constellation. In 1929, the International Astronomical Union (IAU) adopted official constellation boundaries that defined the 88 official constellations that exist today (www.astrol.wise.edu).

When the Earth gradually moves into the winter solstice, the nights become longer and the moonlight wanes into a boundless "black abyss" and the star show begins. Some stars can be viewed with the naked eye, as star clusters are found in the disk of the galaxy largely in the Milky Way. "Many star clusters contain a few hundred loosely arranged stars packed within a diameter that is light years across. Star clusters are bound by their own gravity, and gradually break up from encounters with other stars, and because of 'stretching tides' raised by the galaxy" (www.astronomy.wise.edu). Within the infinite mystery of the Universe, distant orbs of fire light the darkness of the night sky. And the mystery deepens knowing that even some stars shining so brilliantly against the backdrop of blackness are not really there at all; they have burned out light years ago, leaving behind their time warp reflections.

Rocks at the Creek

What is fortunate for the people of Glades County is that the darkness of the wilderness allows the millions of stars in the galaxy to be seen with the naked eye, or enhanced with the use of a telescope. For stargazers who came to the Palmdale campground through 2000 had the opportunity to learn about these beautiful celestial objects as told by Mary and Dow Roland.

The campground was re-leased in 2004 to new proprietors and the stargazing ended.

13

REVIVAL!

❖

1999–2002

THE HISTORIC PALMDALE GENERAL STORE IS PREPARED TO RE-OPEN—JUNE 1999

Red paint splashed up and down tired old beams giving a new life to the Palmdale General Store as proprietor, Deborah Fraga and her crew, soon-to-be-residents, began the revival of the store in preparation for an anticipated opening at the end of July.

Deborah, whose contagious enthusiasm to provide a much-needed general store for Palmdale, greeted a continuous stream of people stopping by to find out when the store will open. Palmdale residents, Jackie and James Garman were one of the first early morning visitors hoping the store was open after being closed for more than a year. When Deborah announced a hoped for opening at the end of July, Jackie happily exclaimed, "that a lot of people can't wait, because now everyone has to run to LaBelle to get anything!"

Bo Roberts, long time Palmdale resident, is ever-present in offering his assistance to return life to the town with the opening of the General Store. Roberts met Deborah's husband, Paul, through their mutual interest in piloting "ultra-light" planes hangared at Ray Hendry's Sabal Palm Campground off Mainstreet and Broadway. Since Paul Fraga was flying into Palmdale most every weekend to offer ultra light rides for $25.00 a half-hour at the Campground, Deborah decided they needed a local place to buy groceries and other items. Thus, the Palmdale General Store will provide general merchandise, camping/fishing/hunting supplies, cigarettes, beer/wine, ice as well as good old home cooking and lots of hospitality from the Fragas, her partners Rose Santos and Paul Vasquez and the ever present Bo Roberts. A buffet breakfast will be served from 4 a.m. with lunch/dinner, deserts/ice-cream and other specialties including pizza for the kids until closing at 11 p.m. seven days a week. To assist Deborah and Paul in actualizing their dream to make the Palmdale Store a general meeting place for residents to socialize over a good cup of coffee or a cold bottle of beer, Bo Roberts volunteered to coordinate a special local arts and crafts section in the store. Anyone who wants to place his or her consignment items in the store has the opportunity. Residents who make homemade jams/jellies/honey, handmade arts/crafts, Seminole jewelry or other items and wish to have shelf space, are invited to display their wares.

Deborah's endless plans to revive the traditional "old country store" feeling in the historical atmosphere also includes the fresh touch of an outdoor cafe under a shaded veranda in front of the store. Even the old red caboose will eventually receive long overdue attention, with Deborah's creative ideas to add another possible entertainment center.

For the people of Palmdale, who want to host a party at the store, birthdays, wedding reception or "coffee klatch," Deborah, her Boca Raton cook and crew will create a discount menu especially for the occasion.

To further the hometown atmosphere, Deborah would like to offer live musical entertainment for weekend visitors. guitar players, singers, banjo artists or string bands that often entertain at the Sabal Palm Campground, will have another place to provide their musical talent. The convenience store will sell newspapers and magazines for those who want to drop in to escape the heat, relax with a cool soda and catch up with the news of the day. A weekend "farmer's market" for local growers to present their harvests along the heavily traveled U.S. 27 is another opportunity for area residents available at the new Palmdale General Store. Deborah says she is willing to try out new ideas that will focus on the services visitors want. She envisions the Palmdale General Store as a central meeting place for everyone to enjoy. She encourages those who have ideas to stop in a talk with her, Paul and Bo Roberts.

Soon, the many truckers who used to always stop for a rest in Palmdale will return when the doors to the Palmdale General Store re-open. The increased business to the town will help link Palmdale residents to other job opportunities by creating a central network of information. Bo Roberts will also maintain a bulletin board where people can post upcoming events, job opportunities, items for sale and business cards. The opening of the store will generate new lifeblood to the town and attract other business interests with the successful operation the Fragas' anticipate as experienced proprietors.

To promote local interests in the area, travelers along U.S. 27 will know exactly where to rent a canoe for Fisheating Creek, when they see Ray Hendry's canoes lining the storefront. Also, wilderness tour guides and naturalists, Dow and Mary Roland, can be contacted through the store for swamp forest walks, wilderness van tours to discover the beauty of Everglades birds, tropical plants for photographic excursions.

Ultra light rides by experienced pilots Bo Roberts and Paul Fraga, who both teach ultra light pilot classes, can be arranged at the store for a breathtaking 30 minute nature tour over the tops of the winding cypress forest weaving along Fisheating Creek.

A host of entertainment and special events are all in the planning stages, but the most important business at hand is providing the much needed groceries and supplies for Palmdale residents. The Fragas' have leased the store for two years, and as success builds, the two are considering the purchase of the store that would allow them to undertake the huge expense necessary to put in gas pumps.

The hospitality, warmth, excitement, smiles and sincere interest the Fragas', Bo Roberts and partners, Rose and Paul are investing in the Palmdale General Store are a much welcome beginning on a new page in Palmdale's history on the Tin Lizzie Trail to the Garden of Eden.

FLY LIKE AN EAGLE IN AN ULTRA LIGHT

Have you ever wanted to live a childhood fantasy of soaring like an Eagle, feeling the wind in your face, lifting you high above the clouds? This fantasy is a real possibility at Palmdale's newest business venture from the airfield at Ray Hendry's Sabal Palm Campground.

Bo Roberts is ready to take off in his ultra-light at Hendry's Campground

Paul Fraga and Bo Roberts, two experienced pilots, have brought the thrill of flying above the winding corridors of Fisheating Creek in a two seater plane called an "Ultra-Light." For $25.00, Paul or Bo will give the passenger a "bird's eye" view at 2 to 3,000 feet above the breathtaking beauty of wilderness frontier. The 1/2 hour ride begins with the "roll-out" from the hangar of one of the two, Max Air Drifter Ultra Lights. The plane weighs approximately 320 pounds. The passenger is secured safety into the seat behind the pilot, and a helmet is worn. Fraga, a licensed Basic Flight Instructor (BFI) and an FAA approved ultra light pilot with more than ten years of ultra light experience, says that flying in an ultra light is "safer than driving a car down U.S. 27." Some of the safety features on board include radio communication, a back up tank of fuel, navigation, cell phone and a Ballistic Recovery System (BRS)—a plane parachute.

How does the ultra light "take off" and fly with a single propeller mounted in the rear? Fraga says they build the ultra light with a propeller at the back with a 581 Rotax engine that pushes the air back and pulls the plane forward. The air speed reaches about 65 miles per hour. Roberts, who has more than 40 years of pilot experience in all types of planes, says the ultra-light is powered by one of the most reliable engines and is easy to control. Roberts says the Ultra Light can travel about 3 1/2 hours on a tank of gas. "Matter of fact," Fraga adds, "in April of 1999, a colleague recently flew 61,000 miles from Argentina to the United States in an ultra light. He stopped only 31 times to refuel."

Fraga (who is also the husband of Deborah Fraga, proprietor of the soon-to-open Palmdale General Store) and Roberts are initiating the first Palmdale Chapter of the Ultra Light Association, part of the Experimental Aircraft Association (EAA) out of Eskosher, Wisconsin. What sparked Fraga's interest to add the ultra light pilot's license to his other credentials as a Kung Fu Master and Massage Therapist was his desire to more closely experience the natural elements and view the beauty of the land. He began flying ultra lights in Coral Springs, and then traveled to the Clewiston airstrip. Bo Roberts and Paul Fraga met as pilots through their shared interest of flying ultra lights. The new chapter of the Ultra Light Association will provide a tourist attraction to Palmdale and the opportunity for residents to experience the thrill of flying. In addition, Fraga offers ultra light pilot Instruction at Ray Hendry's Sabal Palm Campground. When the 10-hour course is completed, including books, intensive flight training, a solo flight and FAA test, you can become an ultra light pilot. The total cost: $600.00. Fraga said that under FAA Code 103, you do not have to have a regular pilot's license to become an ultra light pilot.

The Palmdale Ultra Light Association began a kick-off celebration May 22, 1999, when thirteen planes from all over Florida came to the "Fly-In." On July 1st and 2nd another "Fly-In" occurred with a helicopter arriving from Ft. Myers, and many other types of aircraft participating in the event. There were helicopter and ultra light rides, blue grass music, dancing, a barbecue and a pilots meeting. The event attracted people from all over the area and state.

Every Saturday and Sunday, Bo Roberts and Paul Fraga can be found at the campground hangar for anyone who wants to soar the skies. If not now, when, will you fulfill those childhood dreams especially when it is possible to do so right in Palmdale!

2000—THE PALMDALE GENERAL STORE AND CAFÉ OPENS

The Palmdale General Store and Café opens! The old 1900's two story wooden building that houses the general store and café reflects the true pioneering spirit of Palmdale's history. The Palmdale General Store and Café is a revival of Everglades frontier charm; original wooden shelves stocked with groceries, supplies and the mouthwatering aroma of Breakfast, Lunch and Dinner meals being prepared by Chef Paul, guaranteed to satisfy the hungriest appetite.

The new proprietors, Debra and Paul Fraga, Rose Santos and Paul Vazquez, along with the tireless efforts of Bo Roberts, have swept out the cobwebs, stocked the shelves with a variety of items, refinished wooden counters and tables, and added an All American Menu unmatched on Highway 27. On the Saturday before the big opening day, the hard working team, along with daughter Michelle Fraga, took a much needed coffee break on the outside veranda to talk about the family style atmosphere and food of the Palmdale General Store and Café. Between conversations, travelers along U.S. 27 stopped in with questions and praise for the long awaited opening of Palmdale's only store and café. It was Bo Roberts, who inspired the regeneration of the store, when he became friends with ultra-light pilot/instructor Paul Fraga.

Deborah Fraga, quickly realized that when she visited Palmdale, there was no place to buy food or have a bite to eat, thus, the idea of re-opening the store was a "dream" that became a reality. The enthusiasm of the group is contagious! Paul described some of the breakfast, lunch and dinner specials he is creating with a special flare for taste tempting dishes available during store hours: 5 a.m.–9 pm. Monday through Thursday; 5 a.m.–11 p.m. Friday and Saturday, and 6 a.m.–9 p.m. on Sunday. Paul, an accomplished Chef, who was attracted to the wilderness beauty of Palmdale, says the All American Breakfast buffet with the traditional eggs, bacon/sausage, grits, hash browns, homemade biscuits, and fresh brewed coffee will satisfy the hearty appetite of everyone. But, if you want even more, the breakfast menu offers pancakes, waffles, juices and other side dishes. Lunch and dinner will include a "special" each day, with Gatorama providing a discount coupon at the Café for those who visit that attraction two miles south on U. S. 27. Paul has also added to the menu the favorite exotic Everglades dishes of fresh gator tail and turtle. For the big and little kids alike, pizza and pop are available daily.

On Friday and Saturday night the store sparkles along the roadside with the soft veranda lights and a variety of live music for dining and entertainment. Palmdale residents and visitors can drop in for a meal with the option to sit out on the breezy veranda surrounded by antiques and rafters of hanging flower baskets. Debra is opening the door for local musicians to provide dining patrons with entertainment as a special weekend attraction.

The family style atmosphere is carried throughout the cozy theme of the whole store. A special "Glades Artist" section is rapidly filling with consignment items of all kinds provided by creative local artists and crafters. Colorful fringed western shirts, hand made stuffed dolls, crochet items, paintings, jams/jellies, beaded bracelets/necklaces and ceramics fill the section set aside to display and sell local handmade art. Gatorama is also providing items for sale ranging from Alligator heads to other unique Glades motif items and charms.

The once empty store is now fully stocked with beer, wine, cigarettes, camping goods, ice, sodas, canned goods, sandwich meats, coffee, milk, sugar and just about any other essential item. If there are suggestions for particular selections that you do no see available, Rose will do her best to provide it, just let her know.

Fulfilling a special role as a "community center," the Palmdale General Store offers a unique $1.00 book exchange for those avid novel readers like Mamie Boyce on Easy Street. Debra and Rose have a basket full of books that anyone can exchange for the nominal price of $1.00; or just purchase a book for $2.00. Besides all of these special services, the Palmdale General Store and Café have brochures on wildlife nature tours, information on hunting seasons on the new Wildlife Management Area, The Glades County Democrat for sale, and a bulletin board where Palmdale residents and visitors can post upcoming events and news.

For the adventuresome, you can also sign up at the store for an Ultra-light flight or lessons taught by Bo Roberts and Paul Fraga at Hendry's Sabal Palm Campground. If you want to keep your head out of the clouds for now, you can rent a canoe for a scenic, leisure trip down Fisheating Creek. The enthusiasm of the new proprietors for keeping the traditional Everglades theme and trying out new unique ideas for everyone to enjoy, is inspiring. Their desire to get to know the people of Palmdale and provide residents and visitors with a place to hang their hat amongst friends is an important priority of Debra, Rose and the two Pails.

Just like in the old days, the Palmdale General Store and Café provides a long needed place to buy supplies, and a place where people can look forward to sitting down with family and friends over a good meal, hot coffee or cold beer to enjoy the camaraderie in a warm atmosphere. The Palmdale General Store and Café is a new beginning in Palmdale, a revival of the old town Spirit. Who knows what other new ideas may evolve when friends get together at the Palmdale Store and Café.

Palmdale is no longer a ghost town. The once darkened storefront and boarded windows now light up the night sky along the lone Highway 27, welcoming visitors into the warmth of the Palmdale General Store and Café's cozy surroundings. Once again the chatter of people, music and the wafting aroma of burgers and fries drift into the night air, an invitation to stop in for a visit, some refreshment and a good down home meal.

The Palmdale Store and Café is a welcome new beginning in the historic frontier town on the Tin Lizzie Trail to the Garden of Eden. It marks the hope for the rebirth of Palmdale in its future.

The Palmdale General Store and Café shut down in 2002 and did not re-open.

Photo: *Courtesy of Bud Adams, The Adams Ranch, Ft. Pierce, Florida*

14

"WHEN YOU'RE UP TO YOUR BUTT IN ALLIGATORS, IT'S SOMETIMES HARD TO REMEMBER WHY YOU ENTERED THE SWAMP IN THE FIRST PLACE"

As you drive along U.S. Highway 27 from Moore Haven, you bypass miles of Everglades prairie, the Peeples' ranch, Lykes Brothers working cattle spread, and a small pond where white-crowned eagles are seen soaring high above the clouds prowling the terrain for prey. The highway curls through flatland pastures where young calves cleave together beneath the widespread shade of myrtle trees, escaping the piercing summer sun. Humid heat spins off the revolving rubber of 18 wheelers swirling colored vapor off the oil slick highway in their wake as they crisscross the wilderness packing crates of Florida oranges and Belle Glade produce to points north and out of the peninsula. The semis roar past the flanks of motorists traveling miles across sparse prairie where time slows down. The highway traveler settles into the languid lull of still life scenery passing by along the old Tin Lizzie Trail.

Many years ago along this same highway, then State Road 25, the traveler was greeted and, often entertained, by (now visually absent) hand-carved messages perched atop tree totems luring tourists to the Cypress Knee Museum. Curiosity could not help but be aroused about the man who created, carved, and mounted these original wooden advertisements along a winding road leading to a mysterious Everglades outpost. The tall, slender signposts have long disappeared from the roadside as well as the cypress knee workshop that attracted worldwide visitors.

The dilapidating Cypress Knee Museum, slowly deteriorating across the highway was invaded by thieves who robbed many of its ancient cypress sculptures as the old building sinks into the Earth.

Before the option to relocate the cabbage palm homestead was exercised, attorney David Guest, of the Earth Justice Defense Fund, said there were many examples in the United States where historic sites have been successfully relocated to other areas and remained in tact as a tourist attraction. At the time, worn and spent, Tom Gaskins, Jr. had lost interest in preserving the residential structures as a tourist attraction when it was relocated to Venus (Tasmania).

The legal harangue, fought in court over ten years, made national news calling attention to the growing national concern of preserving the heritage of disappearing cultures.

In Palmdale's legacy to carve a viable economy from its natural treasures, the Cypress Knee Museum reflected the indomitable spirit of early pioneers' tireless pursuit to memorialize its rich cultural heritage and prevent Palmdale's extinction on the edge of the Everglades.

Palmdale, Florida, (140 miles north of Miami on U.S. 27) molded onto grouted streets is a motley mix of trailers, manufactured home, and houses interspersed between thickly knit palmetto brush and canopies of moss-laden oaks. The township is located in the central portion of Glades County, established in 1901, then part of DeSoto County. The rugged individualists from the north, west and east who macheted through the uncharted swamp in the 1900's, were greeted by slithering water moccasins, diamondback rattlesnakes and black clouds of mosquitoes that challenged the most daunting spirit brimming with high hopes of settling this unconquered terrain.

Today, Palmdale is a virtual ghost town with only the Post Office, the Shady Grove, and Hendry's Campground (the latter provides canoes for the creek and down-home bluegrass gatherings); Gatorama remains open along U.S. 27, the 19 mile stretch of highway to Moore Haven, LaBelle or Lake Placid in any direction.

At Broadway and U.S. 27 is the empty storefront of the Palmdale General Store and its two gas station pumps; the last community gather place. Today, the welcoming sign with its painted ice cream cones slowly rots in the sun and fades into history.

CREEPING URBANIZATION

Life as it was here in the wilderness will never be again. Palmdale is on the verge of being swallowed by urbanization with the peripheral expansion of development from the coasts and north, south from Orlando and Miami. The promise of awakening Mr. Fogg's 1900's dream to create a "Garden of Eden" from the Palmdale Land Company is dormant, but eventually his dream will carry a far greater price tag than the few dollars an acre he sold to prospects from around the world. Yet, the pioneering homesteaders who dared to challenge Nature to live here leave an ancestry and legacy to preserve the natural beauty of the land and a cultural heritage. The reclamation of Fisheating Creek and the surrounding wilderness area is the beginning of a broader conservation plan currently being mapped out by the State in a proposed purchase of an additional 120,000 additional acres of Lykes property.

By 2007, the Muse Community is planned to expand into a "rural village" constructed by Lykes Brothers on their property off SR 29 and CR 731. The village plans to develop some 3,500 residential housing units as part of an 895 acre site that includes 68 acres set aside for commercial usage. The housing project is expected to provide reasonably priced homes for employees of the new Muse elementary school.

In 2001, Glades County population according to the U. S. Census was 10,750 with a 2.6% growth in one year and a 39.3% growth over ten years versus the State of Florida's ten year growth of 23.5%. The total land area of Glades County is 774 square miles. The trend for inland growth from the coasts is already a fact. But, there is only so much land and "blue gold" water. Crunching land into smaller parcels to house people and developing an infrastructure of roads, water, sewer will increase traffic, noise, light pollution and inevitably the gradual extinction of the Glades wilderness.

In 2004, two other major construction projects were proposed in Hendry County near LaBelle that outlines plans for 674 residential unites, a golf course and amenities. Near the Lee County line, a more than 500 acre planned residential community is on the drawing board. An approximate total of more than

4,700 acres of development will add tax roll income with an average increase of 2.5 people per household or an additional 3,000 new residents to the area that is growing at a rate of more than 10% per year.

In 2004, Glade's County's had a population of 10,576; there were 1,487 individuals living below the poverty level. In order to preserve the wilderness and create jobs for the residents, creative and innovative eco-tourism development is a question that is also on the drawing boards yet to be strategically resolved. For Palmdale, the solution is a question mark that affects the conservation of a rich cultural heritage and one of Florida's most remote, beautiful, pristine areas.

Governor Jeb Bush created the Rural Economic Development Initiative (REDI), an initiative the Governor states is an effort "to improve the quality of life in Florida's urban cores and depressed rural areas." Patrick Hadley heads the Office of Urban Opportunity within the Governor's Office. Hadley previously served as the founder and executive director of MAD DADS (Men Against Destruction, Defending Against Drugs and Social-disorder) of Greater Ocala.

The separate REDI legislation is a multi-agency initiative focusing the state and regional agencies on problems that affect economic viability or rural communities. REDI is designated to work with local governments, and organizations to find ways to balance environmental and growth management issues with local needs. In 1999–2000 the state budgeted $2 million for loans to assist rural communities in building the infrastructure for development. "Infrastructure" is defined as the "fundamental facilities and systems serving a country, city, or area as transportation and communication systems, power plants and schools." Urban developers require an infrastructure to be established by local governments in order to develop land and build communities. Creeping urbanization begins with jobs created to serve the infrastructure; retooling the local population's skill set or attracting "ready made" skilled laborers to the area, reframing the local economy based on a new employment base that serves the infrastructure and builds the base for urban development.

POPULATION GROWTH: NO TURNING BACK

The characteristics of an area is determined by past history and future vision. When the cultural heritage is obscured, new cultural ideas take hold. New values are introduced into an old area by new people. Destiny: Political power follows money and vice versa. Glades County is at this threshold in the 21st Century.

Although it is inevitable that time will bring change, new people and fresh dreams, those who lived the legends will always remember Palmdale as the fork of two dusty roads between Arcadia and Lakeport on Florida's old "Tin Lizzie Trail."

15

THE NEW PIONEERS

Since the first Indian agronomists altered the topography in order to sustain a viable food source and economy, agriculture in Glades County and Florida has evolved into a stable and important industry. The story of human modification of the land on a larger scale was further initiated in Florida in the 1800's when Pennsylvania toolmaker Hamilton Disston bought four million acres of Florida lands for a quarter an acre.

He also entered into a drainage contract with the Trustees of the Internal Improvement Fund to reclaim vast areas for human settlement and agriculture. Part of that area was the Caloosahatchee River Valley. In the 1800's his dredges connected Lakes Flirt, Hicpochee and Okeechobee with a 5' by 50' canal for navigation and drainage. With eventual government sponsored projects to build locks and intensive projects to control floods over the land, environmental awareness issues of the Caloosahatchee ecosystem became more apparent. In 1993, the federal government created the South Florida Ecosystem Restoration Task Force to re-integrate the ecosystem of South Florida focusing on the Everglades and surrounding watershed. After a century of modifications, the river ecosystem is becoming understood and the connections between the Caloosahatchee watershed and its neighboring areas.

As Florida's history evolved, the state's economy continued to harvest the fruits of the early Indian economic and cultural heritage remaining strongly supported by the agriculture industry. According to the Glades County Chamber of Commerce agriculture, forestry and fishing make up 27.3% of the total employment in citrus, sugar cane crops and cattle, in contrast to the economic urban development chain extending from South Dade through Palm Beach that has altered the former wilderness and farm areas.

One of today's largest horticulturists/agribusinesses in South Florida is Lykes Bros. Inc. Their property in Highlands and Glades counties spreads over 350,000 acres on one of the largest contiguous ownerships in the State. Lykes grows 22,000 acres of citrus trees throughout Central Florida. They manage the largest pine forest in South Florida and graze more than 22,000 head of cattle, making them the fifth-largest cow-calf operation in the United States. Lykes has been in the sugar cane business since before World War I and they currently grow about 4,000 acres of sugar cane each year. (Florida Department of Agriculture and Consumer Services, 1999). Today's technological advances have evolved the agricultural industry into a major contributor to Florida's economy and present preservation from massive urban development.

As part of the increasing awareness of ecosystem vitality, government agencies now exercise an increased level of regulation and oversight of agriculture. In Glades County, according to the Florida Dept of Agriculture and Consumer Services 1999, Lykes Brothers, one of the largest in agribusiness reports that the corporation's environmental coordinator ensures that the company's operations throughout the state meet or exceed farming regulations. Advanced technology used today in the Lykes citrus groves "is designed to maximize the use of gravity for water control. Excess surface water moves through furrows between the citrus tree beds, flowing down a system of canals into water retention ponds. A series of retention areas filter the water before it leaves the property, usually exceeding the state's water quality standards. The retention areas also ensure the flow of water emulating the pre-construction conditions." The ecology of agriculture and protection of wilderness areas and its ecosystems was advanced in Glades County with the settlement between Lykes and the State of Florida in a $46 million dollar purchase of Lykes property on and surrounding Fisheating Creek. Lykes Brothers sold 18,900 acres along the Creek to the State along with 42,000 acres for a Conservation Easement to be maintained as an environmentally protected area designated for recreational use. Phase I of a Five Phase acquisition plan is almost at its completion and negotiation for future purchase of conservation easements will be part of Phase II (Ft. Center is part of the Phase I Wildlife Management Area). The settlement agreement integrates a move towards preservation of the wilderness as coexisting with present agribusiness economy in Glades County. In other Florida counties, the primary economic source of income, i.e. Dade County, has evolved from an agricultural economy to urban development and its accompanying by-products of increased population, traffic, city lights, pollution, sprawling country clubs with accompanying lakes (that may or may not meet water quality standards), and disappearance of the wilderness.

THE PAST MEETS THE FUTURE

In the rich history of Glades County, the early pioneers plunged into uncharted territory and carved a future in the cattle business, fishing industry, sugar, agriculture, aquaculture and other small businesses that had its roots in the 1800's. The three "R's", roadways, rails and river opened the gateway to the advantageous location of Glades County to central Florida and the United States. The fertile "black gold" soil unique to the Everglades ecosystem provided the resource for economic development and attracted developers and homesteaders from all over Europe and the United States. Many of these early communities, Citrus Center, Hall City have disappeared except for the people who followed their dreams to the area, remained to raise families and create a living from the natural resources. The legacy of the these early pioneers is now in the hands of present generation "new pioneers" who still believe in harvesting a prosperous economic future for Glades County. These "new pioneers" have sprung up in a "grass roots" organization called the Glades County Economic Development Council.

The "new pioneers" in Glades County are continuing the tradition of charting new territory by expanding economic opportunities and planned growth. The Mission of the Glades County Economic Development Council is: To promote quality economic development to benefit the citizenry through positive, professional planning and leadership.

1999: THE ECONOMIC DEVELOPMENT COUNCIL GOALS FOR THE DECADE

On August 18, 1999, more than two dozen Glades County citizens met to formulate a Strategic Management Plan for the future. Glades Electric Cooperative spearheaded the Economic Development Council initiative in an effort to formulate a Mission, Vision, Values, Goals and Objectives for the growth of Glades County. As John Ahern, Chairman of the Economic Development Council comments, "in order to control our own destiny." Mr. Ahern expresses the view that "the time is right for the expansion of 'ecotourism' in Glades County and industrial growth such as the development of an industrial park, presently being considered, that would take advantage of the three R's: railway, roads, and river."

John Ahern—One of the founders of the Glades County Economic Development Council

ECOTOURISM

One of the evolving economic development initiatives worldwide targeted as a potential market in Glades County by the Economic Development Council is "ecotourism." Internet research on "ecotourism" provides insight into the economic opportunities already networking throughout the world. The term "ecotourism" has a broad definition: "Nature tourism, adventure tourism, cultural tourism, educational tourism, and historical tourism. It is a concept that describes a form of development that respects tradition and culture, protects and preserves the environment, educates and welcomes visitors. Ecotourism should also be economically sustainable over the long term." Many books are available on how to establish an "ecotourism" business for entrepreneurs or local governments. For example, recently in Glades County, one cultural heritage preservation project, considered part of "ecotourism" development, was initiated by school children under the guidance of teacher Laura Ahern. As part of an English class project, students recorded interviews with Glades County pioneers, and then presented their reports in Tallahassee. Their effort was in support of establishing Moore Haven's Main Street as a National Historic District that would provide incentive for preservation and restoration of the town's cultural heritage and attract visitors to the area.

With the founding of the Economic Development Council, the first step was to formulate a strategic economic development plan for Glades County. EDC Interim Director, Mike Vinson of Glades Electric Cooperative, invited facilitator Pat Merritt of Atlanta, who has assisted other electric cooperatives in Georgia to develop economic and industrial goals, to work with the Council on similar objectives.

The initial organizational meeting, open to all interested Glades County citizens, included a cross-section of participants from Buckhead Ridge, Muse, Palmdale, Moore Haven, Ortona, Lakeport, the Glades County Chamber of Commerce, the Southwest Florida Regional Council, Glades County School Board, City/County Government and local businesses. At the beginning of the meeting, the facilitator asked everyone to participate in a futuristic exercise. The group was asked to envision the future of Glades County in the year 2009. Some of the "common vision themes" anticipated over the next ten years is the development of eco-tourism, quality jobs, infrastructure improvements, expanded educational opportunities, a lower crime rate, planning and zoning conducive to future development, a countywide communication network and lower taxes.

In order to achieve these visions participants were asked to form small working groups to address present concerns that need to be solved in order to reach the identified objectives. The group then compiled a list of present priorities and goals to tackle as ongoing projects. The priorities include: improving government attitudes, leadership, funding, maintaining enthusiasm and developing marketing strategies. Each of the small groups developed an action plan to address each of the identified concerns. The goals set forth to approach each of the concerns include:

1. Attitude: To work with government agencies, businesses and community organizations to obtain active support in promoting economic development in Glades County.

2. Leadership: Establish a profile for an Executive Director.

3. Funding: Fund a budget by working with local governmental agencies, corporate sponsors, an active membership, state and federal agencies.

4. Maintaining Enthusiasm: Maintain and promote enthusiasm with the Board/community and develop a marketing strategy.

Each group formulated objectives and an action plan to confront these issues as follows:

I. Attitude (Small Group participants: Mike Vinson, Joe Flint, Betty Williams, and Dottie Cook)

  A. Attend meetings of agencies and organizations/local and state.

  B. Publish information on goals, objectives for distribution.

  C. Make quarterly presentations to City, County and Board of Education.

II. Leadership (Small Group participants: Trey Price, Bobby Flanagan, Pat Gormann, and Tom Gaskins)

  A. Hire an Executive Director or a volunteer Executive Director.

    1. Research Hendry and Okeechobee Economic Development Councils.

    2. Develop a job description.

    3. Identify avenues for advertising position by word of mouth, Tallahassee, current residents and newspaper.

III. Budget (Small Group participants: Gary Clark, Greg Warr, John Ahern, and Norm Rynning)

  A. Government agencies (School, City, County).

  B. Bylaws, membership corporate sponsors, homeowner's groups, grant writer.

  C. 501 (c) 3-tax status; Glades attorney; corporate sponsors.

  D. Foundations.

IV. Maintaining Enthusiasm (Small Group participants: Susan Smelley, David Watson, and Patty Register)

  A. Press announcements.

  B. Telephone notification.

C.   Quarterly events to celebrate recognition of accomplishments.

D.   Promote membership by each member recruiting one.

The first strategic planning was viewed by the Council "as the first of many on the road to a prosperous economic development effort. It requires the unrelenting commitment of dedicated citizens and community leaders for true success." Executive Director, Mike Vinson stressed that at this stage "the Council needs on-going financial support of individuals and businesses in Glades County; participation, personal support and commitment. Economic development is not an overnight process. Looking down the road, it will take several years before significant organizational objectives and foundational financial considerations are met. Probably one of our greatest concerns in Glades County is our lack of infrastructure (water, sewer, and a developed industrial park). These things must be addressed and resolved before we can expect to attract substantial growth."

As another effort, Chairman Ahern outlines the Council's collaborative project with Gulf Coast University in Ft. Myers to develop ideas for a Strategic Management Plan. With the assistance of Dr. Robert Walsh, Chairman of the Public Administration Department, Professors Walsh and Geraldo Flowers are teaching a graduate seminar on "Rural Economic Development" as part of the Master's in Public Administration degree focusing on "the theory and practice for planning local economic development in a rural setting. The seminar examines topics such as strategic planning, business development, and institutional approaches for local economic development and human resource management." Dr. Walsh views the department's role in working with the Council "as a resource to guide/ assist in economic development using Glades as the setting to give the subject matter a real world context for the students and to provide some support to Glades County in the process."

The syllabus describes the course objectives as "examining the complexities of local economic development with a theme of providing a base of understanding about local economic development in a rural setting and community-based strategic plan." The course runs through Dec 1, 2000. Graduate students will take on a specific project that may consist of a "study, analysis, or grant proposal in support of Glades County's strategic plan for community or economic development."

Additionally, August 23, 2000, Chairman John Ahern presented a progress report on the Economic Development Council to the Glades County Commission who allocated $15, 0000 to support their continued efforts and the City of Moore Haven designated an additional $5,000.00. Curtis Fry, Executive Director of the Glades County Chamber of Commerce said that they "support economic development in the county by answering all inquires and sending out the Chamber booklet that outlines all of the services and resources in the area. The Chamber contributes to the County's economic development any way they can. We are a member of their Board and have members on the Board. The Chamber also supports the Chalo Nitka festival every year that provides salaries to pay for promotional brochures. The Chamber is at a cross-road, we are looking to hire a new Executive Secretary to help the community by becoming more involved in the economic development needs of Glades County."

FLORIDA GULF COAST UNIVERSITY AND GLADES ECO DEVELOPMENT COUNCIL ON THE MOVE—1999

Florida Gulf Coast University's Public Administration Department and the Glades Economic Development Council are collaborating to explore opportunities for economic development in Glades County. A group of students enrolled in the Master's Degree program in Public Administration are participating in a seminar on "Rural Economic Development" that is focusing on developing a strategic economic development plan in a joint project with the EDC.

On Saturday, November 4th, Dr. Geraldo Flowers, Professor of the course and Dr. Robert Walsh, Chairman of the Department, met in Moore Haven with the Glades EDC to review the focus and progress of the students involved in research and development. Dr. Flowers indicated "that the first step in exploring economic options for the County's development is to collect information on opportunities presently available in Glades County especially from an eco-tourism perspective." Part of the discussion of the group included ideas that would promote the natural assets in Glades County that will bring tourists to the area. The students intend to develop a marketing strategy for print media, a Web page and advertising brochures that depict the natural beauty of the environment, economic opportunities of the strategic location of the County, and the wilderness activities that can create new business ventures and jobs. Dr. Flowers also suggested that a public service commercial be created for local radio stations to "get the message out as to what is available in Glades County to encourage interest in building on what is presently in place."

EDC Chairman John Ahern says that the meeting was productive. They had "an excellent discussion that concluded with the initiation of the first steps of the plan to gather pictures and information to use in the promotional brochures, and Website." Three members of the FGCU graduate students present at the meeting divided up the workload of the project and will report back to the committee at the next meeting, December 2nd in Moore Haven.

Patty Register, Vice President of the EDC believes that "working with Gulf Coast University provides a foundation that the Council is building for the citizens of Glades County to begin educating ourselves on what responsible economic development can be pursued. The EDC hopes to build a common vision with our citizens on determining the best options for economic development. We have plans to bring in consultants to hold townhall meetings to explore ecotourism opportunities that will bring jobs to Glades County. Glades County has so many 'nature based' opportunities that those of us who live here may overlook because we live within this unique natural ecosystem. We need to explore these natural wonders in our own backyard that urban tourists would be willing to pay for to visit. I hope people will attend the townhall meetings with the expectation that they will gain valuable knowledge in order to build eco-based businesses in Glades County."

FLORIDA GULF COAST UNIVERSITY PREPARES GRANT PROPOSAL FOR GLADES COUNTY ECONOMIC DEVELOPMENT—2000

The Economic Development Council headed by Executive Director, Mike Vinson of Glades Electric Cooperative has been working the past several months with graduate students taking a course in "Rural Economic Development" through the Public Administration Department at Florida Gulf Coast University in Ft. Myers. The Council has been collaborating with Gulf Coast students in researching various strategic economic plans that can assist Glades County in developing an expanded economic base to bring jobs and businesses to the area. The Council views strategic planning as the first step towards developing a prospectus of prosperous economic development ideas.

Florida Gulf Coast University's Public Administration department's role in working with the Council is as a resource and guide to assist Glades County through the project and provide an opportunity for students to work in a "real world" context. The Council and the class members have been examining various ideas that will capitalize on the area's natural resources including ecotourism and industrial opportunities that John Ahern, Chairman of the Council describes as focusing on Glades County's three R's: roads, rail and river. The graduate students are in the final phase of completing a proposal for the Glades County Manager and Commissioners.

James Ward, a member of the class is working on a Web Page that will give residents "(1) More access to county offices and information about the Economic Development Council activities; (2) Advertise local activities (i.e. Fishing, restaurants, biking, hunting) that will bring people from surrounding areas into the county." This proposal will be part of a comprehensive proposal for the Website start-up and maintenance that will be presented to the county officials. Ward says their project includes a proposal for half of a matching grant of $15, 000 that can be paid for by FGCU to be used to perform a feasibility study on ecotourism in Glades County." Presently statistical data is being compiled for inclusion in the grant proposal that outlines the population, demographics, and economic status of the County. Mindy Collier of the South Florida Regional planning Council, according to Ward, is working on this aspect of the proposal. Once the grant has been obtained a feasibility study will be conducted to determine the potential financial success of certain types of ecotourism businesses. However, the potential of ecotourism economic development is only one suggested use of the grant proposal funds; a cost benefit analysis is suggested to be performed that will determine if ecotourism business development is the most beneficial use of funds and, additionally, what other economic spin-offs or opportunities are embedded in Glades County that may result in cost effective economic growth.

Information gathered for the Web page development and the economic study will be used to develop marketing brochures on Glades County highlighting its rich cultural history and business opportunities. Although the Glades County Economic Development Council initiated the collaborative effort with Florida Gulf Coast University, the grant proposal is for the comprehensive economic growth of Glades County. EDC members stress the importance of course projects that will be ongoing beyond the length of the semester class. It is anticipated that the proposal will impact the future economic planning and development in Glades County.

GREATER EVERGLADES ECOSYSTEM RESTORATION CONFERENCE
December 11–15 2000

On December 11–15, at the Naples Beach Hotel and Golf Club, the Science Coordination Team, a committee of the South Florida Ecosystem Restoration Task Force and Working Group is hosting an Everglades ecosystem conference called "Defining Success." The purpose of the conference is to "provide a forum for physical, biological and social scientists to share their knowledge and research results concerning Everglades restoration. The objectives are to define specific restoration goals, determine the best approaches to meet these goals, and provide benchmarks that can be used to measure the success of restoration efforts over time."

Presentations by scientists and experts represent a cross section of topics that effect Glades County including Water Quality and Water Treatment Technologies, ("Getting the water right: water quality"); Social and Human Sciences ("Agricultural and environmental economics, land use, economic and demographic trends, planning and community involvement, forecasting, allocation and behavioral models"); Information Systems (Real Time Data Access, WEB access and retrieval); Ecology and Ecological Modeling (Populations and population modeling, indicators of species, sustainable population; invasion of exotic species, community dynamics and succession, wetlands).

Some of the specific topics include: "An Analysis of Changes in Basin-Wide and Farm-Scale Phosphorus Loading from the Everglades Agricultural Area Due to Implementation of Best Management Practices," presented by Randy McCafferty and William Baker, South Florida Water Management District; Water Quality Impact Analysis of Southwest Florida; "Wetland Permitting Alternative on Surface Water Quality," presented by Terry Rice, Florida International University, Dennis Peters and others of the Science Applications International Corporation; "An Assessment of Potential Contaminant Exposures and Effects for Alligators in the Greater Everglades Ecosystem," presented by Timothy Gross, U.S. Geological Survey, Florida Caribbean Science Center.; "Forecasting Human Population of South Florida: The State of the Art and Directions for the Future," presented by Alice L. Clarke, FIU; "Ways to Make Science More Usable for Policy Makers and Managers in Greater Everglades Ecosystem Restoration and Management," presented by Frank J. Mazzotti, University of Florida. ; Environmental Decision making by Stakeholder Consensus, presented by Michael Bauer, National Wildlife Federation.

According to conference organizers, the Everglades "restoration goals stated by the South Florida Ecosystem Restoration Taskforce, are broad in context and short on specifics. In 1989, the Everglades Restoration Conference succeeded in synthesizing what was known concerning the ecology of the Everglades ecosystem and what was needed for restoration. In the intervening years, there have been a number of advances in understanding ecology and history of the Everglades." This conference will work to further define what the restored system will be and how to attain it.

Sessions include speakers from the U.S. Geological Survey, National Oceanographic and Atmospheric Administration, US Fish and Wildlife Service, University of Miami experts on hydrology, and speakers from Duke University's Wetland Center and many more scientists.

EVERGLADES RESTORATION 2004

Evaluating the 2003 progress of Everglades Restoration, a 400-page report was issued, the sixth in an annual series, by the South Florida Water Management District and the Department of Environmental Protection (DEP) on how the water quality in Florida has been improved. A summary of the report indicates that phosphorus levels in the Everglades were reduced based on scientific evaluation with new funds in the amount of $444 million earmarked for further reductions. Additionally, modified farming practices, man-made storm water treatment areas continue to reduce the phosphorous along with mercury concentrations found in wading birds reduced by 60%. Biological controls to eliminate exotic plants and infestation of invasive insects were also indicated as reduced in some areas by 80%. Continued technological innovations and scientific data will be evaluated over the ten year project that began in 2000.

JUNE 2004—EMINENT DOMAIN

Jesse James Hardy, 68, a resident of Golden Gate Estates in Hardy County is the final holdout for the State's acquisition of his 160 acres to include in the 19,000 already purchased in the county for the restoration project. Hardy turned down the State's $4.5 million dollar offer for his property, choosing to hold onto the slash pine, cabbage palm area that encircles his modest home in an area characterized as a "hideout for drug smugglers." Governor Jeb Bush, after more than a year of negotiations asked the Department of Environmental Protection to condemn Hardy's property if he did not accept money or a land swap by the end of the summer. Presently, the State has not initiated the "eminent domain" proceedings empowered to them to obtain property for projects considered to be beneficial to Everglades restoration.

The Everglades plan comprises more than 60 separate projects totaling more than 2.4 million acres of Florida land. It has been called "the world's largest, most important ecological restoration and an ill-conceived boon-doggle."

16

THE LAST WILDERNESS FRONTIER

Glades County will forever be at a crossroad as long as there is land and water. Observing the effects in nearby counties, Glades County could become another industrial development site. In choosing a direction, collaborative effort to find solutions to economic needs that will provide income and employment opportunities to support the county's residents and expand growth that the land can support is a delicate balance. The big question in Florida is not new.

The sunshine state continues to attract thousands of new residents each day with a need for human habitat. The trend of developing managed communities, providing houses and jobs has drawbacks that cannot be reversed. Piggybacking on development is just what the word implies "change." The perks include advanced technology, million dollar country clubs, sprawling golf courses, shopping centers, light pollution, sewage treatment plants, noise and crime. But, people have to live somewhere.

The quality of life issues are vital to the human spirit. The preservation of Florida's indigenous natural species of plant, birds, and wildlife are an important factor in designing communities; they cannot be replaced. The visionaries of Glades County's leadership will mold the thinking, direction, development, and preservation of what exists in the present. Perhaps the leaders, observing the urbanization infiltrating from the coasts into Glades County, can find solutions to economic needs that will provide income and employment to support the county's residents and growth that the land can support.

Look around, capture the essence of the trees looming in the sky, the smell of the swamp, the canopy of stars, the crimson sunsets over the prairie, the golden silence over which can be heard the whispered chatter of the swallow-tailed kites soaring on the wind currents in an azure blue sky. This is what is beholden to the last wilderness area in Glades County, Florida.

THE PALMDALE
Palmdale, Florida

THE BRIDGE AT PALMDALE

EPILOGUE
"BLUE GOLD" WATER

The Earth is the only planet we know that survives by water. Eighty-percent of the Earth's surface is water, our brains 75 percent. As we grow older we "dry out" and become 50 percent water. Water is the content of our cells. Of the 11 gallons of water in the average body, 6 1/2 make up the fluid in cells. Water is the earth's thermostat and human body regulator of heat. Water stores heat and lowers body temperature. Fresh water amounts to 3.7 percent of the world's supply, mostly stored in glaciers, ice caps and the atmosphere. The limited amount of water available to human beings is drawn from wells, streams and lakes comprising .0007 percent of the global water supply.

Global water use has increased rapidly over the past 70 years. There are so many more people using water drawn from underground aquifers, artesian wells, rivers, streams and lakes that by 2025 at the present rate of consumption, 90% of the freshwater in developed nations will be used up. When fresh water aquifers near the ocean are pumped out, it is often replaced by saline water seeping in. Mammals and plants cannot survive with salt-water pollution in ground drinking water.

Besides a water shortage crisis, population growth and increased consumption degrade water quality available, contaminated by life-threatening substances including chemicals from industry, agriculture, and household products spilling into the fresh-water supply. Further, hormone and antibiotic laced animal and human waste seeping into storage basins recycling into human use, creates potentially devastating immune, endocrine and reproduction system disorders that only now, researchers are identifying as water related.

In Florida, sprawling golf courses "planted" in former orange groves are growing rapidly in the landscape of housing developments bearing namesakes that do not resemble their identity such as "Orange Blossom Estates," or "Cypress Hammock Community," with nary a fragrant orange or cypress tree in sight. Golf courses with its chemical use to maintain lush greens are an environmental detriment, but golf is a big business contributing more than $49 billion a year to the U.S. economy. In the United States, golf courses cover more than 1.7 million acres and soak up almost 4 billion gallons of water daily. They also use pesticides and fertilizers that contribute to water pollution. In 1994, the University of Iowa's, College of Medicine, found an unusually high number of deaths from certain cancers among farm works and pesticide applicators working on 618 gold courses in the United States including brain cancer and non-Hodgkin's lymphoma.

The expansive population growth of 1,000 people a day moving to Florida that piggybacks on the number one industry of tourism and recreation is creating an expensive concern to solve environmental problems.

But the perpetuation of future problems is not contained in large urban areas as sprawling transportation networks criss-cross the state creating new hubs of development extending north, south, east and west. The first step in re-structuring a rural community is through the development of a new economic infrastructure that provides services such as water, sewage treatment, roads to support industrial growth offering minimum wage jobs that promise a future by re-training rural workers, who may be only have worked as cowboys their entire life, into the "new economy" through job transition.

Moving along the urban coastal fringes like a bullet train towards Glades County is the threat of rural heritage and cultural extinction, including loss of wetlands, endangered species, and habitat, in exchange for air, water and light pollution. It is a high premium to pay for an urban-based economy.

A positive move in the current of events is that a few governmental groups in South Florida are discouraging the proliferation of urban sprawl. During the 60's and 70's, the growth philosophy of the urbanizing areas along the lower eastern coast of Florida was to accommodate growth by pushing development west toward the Everglades counties virtually threatening to absorb rural populations of their distinct character and history. giving way to auto dependent suburban residents. Although Glades County has only 1% of the land area utilized for urban land uses, with nearly two thirds owned by Lykes Brothers, growth issues from the east and west coast are already impacting the county with the addition of Governor Jeb Bush's Rural Economic Development Initiative (REDI) in 2000. The program provides funds for rural diversity including monies to determine if a county has the ability to provide infrastructure to support maximum projected growth under its existing comprehensive plan, or is the development for industrial sites ripe to turn from an agricultural or budding ecotourism economy into an industrial area.

The transformation of urban sprawl into what is termed "quality development patterns," is under the auspices of local governments, the South Florida Water Management District and the South Florida Regional Planning Council. The SFWMD and the SFRFC is representative of a board appointed to make decisions for the majority, in lieu of "by the majority" of people whose future lifestyle, economic stability, land/water use will parceled by their decisions.

In 2004, at Ortona, the Glades County Enterprise Zone Development Agency (EXDA) moved to generate more property tax per square foot by attracting industrial development, proposing more favorable future land use zoning. The proposal included changing a residential zone to industrial with the Governor's approval through the Office of Tourism, Trade and Economic development, not an "oxymoron" grouping of terms in the governmental office.

Funds available for tourism can be easily tied in with industrial development as indicated by the Governor's office handling economic development. Enterprise zones are slated as economic areas targeted inside counties for industrial sites.

FACTS TO PONDER: WATER USAGE IN AMERICA

2 gallons to bush one's teeth each day
4 gallons to flush a toilet one
20 gallons to hand wash dishes; 13 gallons to put dishes through an automatic washer.
1, 800 gallons to refine one barrel of oil.

Water is life and we are the caretakers of the well. As water wears away the stone, and nurtures the creatures on Earth, it also is the first to "wither." When the land is turned to cement highways, trees cut down for development replacing indigenous species with ornamentals not adapted to Florida's unique climate the land and environment are altered, including evaporation and condensation of the water cycle.

When we lose intimacy with the natural world, cloned in air-conditioned cement blocks most of our lives, we become unaware and ignorant of the water related, live-giving processes we depend upon to survive. We then seem shocked, as if caught off guard when our insulated capsules are disturbed by a new culture that uproots and transplants the old ways and values, perhaps not in any better or familiar way, but more prolific and entrenched then life breath of the natural world.

Trees, plants and the habitat are all part of the water life cycle. The nurturing of life, blue gold water, exists as a non-sustainable and non-renewable entity when siphoned from the earth's stores before it can replenish itself through the natural processes of evaporation, condensation, rain and storage in the heart of the earth's reservoirs.

Besides the land, the blue-gold water that whispers silently over and through the underground primordial porous limestone beneath Glade's County is the custodian of life-giving forces. In the last of the vanishing wilderness areas in Florida, the wildlife cannot speak out, it is only the human guardians who enjoy the pristine beauty, quiet and star clustered skies that have a voice in preserving Nature's wonders in a healthy environment.

Man, when surrounded by inanimate objects, becomes sterile. The mind and body replenish, just like the soil, the plants and other animals through the touch of Nature. Transcendentalist Henry David Thoreau became a symbol in his quiet revolution at Walden by rejecting society's "spin" on how he should live his life, thus, he grew vegetables instead of working in a factory. Though he attended Harvard University, he was an unconventional scholar as reflected in his life and writings, expressing a willed integrity to conscientiously refuse or accept the will of the government or others upon his own life direction and purpose. He believed in inner freedom and the ability for human beings to build their own lives. He was a supreme individualist and championed the human spirit against materialism and social conformity.

In 1845, he built himself a small cabin on the shores of Walden Pond, near Concord, Massachusetts to live in eloquent solitary and close harmony with Nature. He remained there for more than two years, "living deep and sucking out all the marrow of life." He supported himself by growing tomatoes, surveying and doing odd jobs nearby. He observed Nature and wrote about what he learned.

Thoreau expressed the rural values that are often dismissed today by those who believe in the dominant contrasting value of the "fast lane," chasing dollars, bigger and better, richer phenomena. Yet, when there is little breathing room, land and water left, replaced by ornamental, lifeless surroundings, man's sprit will evaporate just like the water. There are some intangible unsustainable life-giving forces that money cannot buy including, health, time and human relations.

Man's time is limited as are all creatures upon which we share this space in the universe. We are not alone, although we may seem alone. Our world is alive with the smallest and largest insects and beasts, from the tiny thriving anthill whose community has burrowed its nest in the Everglades sand, to the iridescent glow from a Florida black bear's eyes hollowing out shadows in the night in search of food. Imagine our world as we would make it: Sprayed lawns, cement houses, artificial lights, gated communities, traffic, pollution gray horizons, the smell of chemical fumes and the night so bright with lights that the stars die. What future do we choose to carve about how we choose to live?

"What is man without the beasts? If all the beasts were gone, men would die from a great loneliness of spirit. For whatever happens to the beasts, soon happens to man. All things are connected."

—Chief Seattle, Suqamish Chief, 1854

Photo: *Courtesy of Bud Adams, The Adams Ranch, Ft. Pierce, Florida*

0-595-32557-2

Printed in the United States
22079LVS00001B/307-339